The
Principles
God
RESPECTS

Living by Faith is the Key to Success

REV. PRAYER KENNETH OBADONI

WESTBOW°
PRESS
A DIVISION OF THOMAS NELSON
& ZONDERVAN

WestBow Press books may be ordered through booksellers or by contacting:
WestBow Press
A Division of Thomas Nelson & Zondervan
1663 Liberty Drive
Bloomington, IN 47403
www.westbowpress.com
1 (866) 928-1240

ISBN: 978-1-4908-4103-8 (sc)
ISBN: 978-1-4908-4102-1 (hc)
ISBN: 978-1-4908-4104-5 (e)

Library of Congress Control Number: 2014910893

Printed in the United States of America.

WestBow Press rev. date: 06/23/2014

Contents

Dedication

This book is affectionately dedicated to my mother-in-law, Mrs. Josephine Enetoduaganeju Adodo nee Ugborogho, for guiding me through this project with her years of experience in ministry and working in the vineyard of God.

Acknowledgements

First of all, I want to thank God for giving me the ability to put this together, special appreciation to all the pastors, friends, and entire members of our ministry worldwide for every support and prayers.

To my editor Dr. Bonnie Harvey God bless you for your labour of love in editing my manuscript The Principles God Respects.

Finally, my heartfelt appreciation to my wife I say thank you for making it worthwhile.

I Love you all and stay blessed.

Introduction

"Living by Faith is the Key to Success"
"And without faith it is impossible to
please God because anyone
who comes to God must believe that he exists and that he
rewards those who earnestly seek Him."
(Hebrews 11:6, NIV)

Whether you are a young believer or have walked with the Lord for years, God expects you to walk in faith—that is, to walk according to the principles God sets forth in Hebrews 11:6. The important idea to remember here is to believe God exists and to keep Him foremost in your mind and actions. He cares for you, but at the same time, unless you exercise faith (trust and confidence) in Him and His Word, your Christian life will not prosper as it should.

Although there are many ways you can live for the Lord and serve Him, unless you perform these acts by faith, they won't count for much in your Christian life. In fact, Hebrews 11:6 spells out what God requires of us: that is, to live and walk by faith. The great reformer, Martin Luther, discovered this truth back in 1517 when God showed him how to obtain peace with God.

Luther was a Catholic monk who spent hours on his knees trying to find forgiveness for his sins. Then, the Lord revealed Romans 1:17 to him: "The just shall live by faith." From that moment on, Luther knew his sins were forgiven and he had peace with God.

God began to stress the life of faith with Abraham in Genesis 12 when he called Abraham to "Leave your country, your people, and your father's household and go to a land that I will show you" (Genesis 12:1). {Abraham's call continues over several chapters in Genesis including God's promise of an heir in Genesis 15—even though Abraham was already 75 years old.}Verse seven shows Abram's faith when it says, "Abram believed the Lord, and he credited it to him as righteousness."

The New Testament tells us over and over to have the faith of Abraham in passages like Romans 4:2-3, Galatians 3:6, and James 2:23. Since as believers, we are the seed of Abraham and he is "our father" in the faith, let us endeavor to follow Christ walking by faith with every fiber of our being. In each of the chapters that follow, we will discuss different aspects of faith and how the believer can confidently walk in each one triumphantly.

CHAPTER ONE

Serving God

"Decide today whom you will obey.
Will it be the gods of your ancestors
beyond the Euphrates or the gods of
the Amorites here in this land? But
as for me and my family, we will
serve the Lord."
(Joshua 24:15, TLB)

Moses' death at the end of Deuteronomy paved the way for his aide, Joshua, to come forth and lead the children of Israel into the Promised Land of Canaan. God promised his people in (Deut. 28:1-2) "If thou shalt hearken diligently unto the voice of the Lord thy God, to observe and to do all his commandments... the Lord thy God will set thee on high above all nations of the earth."

The list includes all manner of material blessings coming to God's chosen people including living in houses they didn't build and using vineyards they didn't plant. Joshua's orders at the outset of the book of Joshua are: "Possess the land, which the Lord your God gives you to possess it" (Joshua 1:11). At this point, the Israelites were still on the other side of the Jordan, but

1

preparations were taking place for them to cross over into the land God had promised Abraham hundreds of years earlier. In fact, Abraham's son, Isaac, was called the "child of promise."

When the priest carried the ark of the covenant (the symbol of God's presence) across the Jordan River, the river dried up allowing them to cross on dry land. Soon, all the men, including the soldiers, were told about their fighting at the city of Jericho. Their fighting was to be "a fight of faith" as Joshua ordered them to march around the city once a day for seven days—not saying a word! On the seventh day, they were to march around the city seven times blowing trumpets and the shofar—and shouting praises to God, which they did. In response, the thick city walls of Jericho fell by faith. The soldiers had not used any weapons except the weapon of faith in God's Word. God also spared Rahab and her family because she hid the spies.

After Jericho fell, the soldiers marched onto Ai, expecting an easy victory. The leaders said, "Let not all the people go up; but let about two or three thousand men go up and smite Ai... for they are but few" (Joshua 7:3). Only about three thousand soldiers marched on Ai, but because of Achan, an Israelite soldier, they were soundly defeated. Achan had stolen a garment from the Amorites (which they were told to destroy), and had buried it along with a wedge of gold and two hundred shekels of silver, which he had also stolen. Achan and his entire family were stoned to death, as well as his oxen, sheep and cattle, his goods, and his entire family. When he had dealt with Achan's sin, Joshua and his family proceeded to destroy the city of Ai according to God's instructions.

The following chapters of the book of Joshua deal with Joshua, as the leader, parceling out the land to the twelve tribes of Israel. Each tribe had to "take" its land—that is, free the land from their enemies, most of whom were Amorites. All of this was accomplished by faith, and through God's promises to them;

although none of the tribes freed their land entirely from its inhabitants.

Joshua challenged the tribes in his closing address to determine who they would serve: Would it be the Egyptian gods, like the sun god, - "Re,-" and -"Osiris,-" ruler of the realm of the dead; or would the Israelites serve the gods of the Amorites,: like one of the Baals that practiced fertility rites and child sacrifice?.

It's interesting that Joshua gave the people a choice about whom they wanted to serve. The Israelites were supposed to conquer their land and its inhabitants and tell them about the one true God and not to succumb to worthless idols.

God gives us a choice, too. But in the New Testament our choice is often between God and mammon (money). As Jesus said in the Sermon on the Mount: "No man can serve two masters: for either he will hate the one and love the other; or else he will hold to the one, and despise the other. You cannot serve God and mammon" (Matt. 6:2).

Not until the time of King David did the Israelites conquer the majority of their enemies although they lived in the Promised Land. We, too, as believers must persevere and continue to defeat our enemies. Some of these enemies are doubt, discouragement, and unbelief—and, of course, pride. God will help us, though, as we look to Him like Joshua did in Joshua 1:8 when he proclaimed: "This book of the law shall not depart out of thy mouth; but thou shalt meditate therein day and night, that thou mayest observe to do according to all that is written therein: for then thou shalt make thy way prosperous, and then thou shalt have good success."

Norman Vincent Peale, a minister of the gospel, illustrated a person who chose to serve God. "With his charming accessibility, good humor and matchless style as a story teller," Norman Vincent Peale could captivate any audience. [1] His charm and message arrived on the American scene following -"the Great Depression-"

and just before World War II began. People needed some new hope and optimism to carry them through this uncertain time.

The timing of Norman Vincent Peale's birth appeared perfect for the task given to him. Norman arrived in the home of Anna and Clifford Peale on May 31, 1898, in the small Ohio town of Bowersville. Although Clifford was a Methodist minister, he had earlier trained to become a medical doctor so he and Anna decided to deliver their first born without the benefit of other helping personnel.

By the time Norman was seventeen, and ready for college, he had lived in seven Ohio locations and more than a dozen Methodist parsonages because of his father's call to different churches as a Methodist minister.

The Peale family moved to yet another church in Greenville, Ohio, when Norman was twelve. They moved again three years later, when he turned fifteen. In spite of his many moves, young Norman finished the full high school curriculum, including courses in Latin, German, English, history, math, and science in 1916, from Belle Fontaine High School. During this time he picked up part-time jobs like delivering newspapers and even a job as a door-to-door salesman.

Every summer, Norman attended the Methodist Camp meeting center in Lakeside, Ohio. The Peale family was at the camp meeting when news came about the beginning of World War I. The year included the news that the state of Ohio defeated Prohibition by an eighty-three thousand- vote majority.

Norman began his college career in 1916 at Ohio Wesleyan, a Methodist institution where he received scholarship help. Ohio Wesleyan was a thorough-going Methodist School that prohibited smoking, drinking, and dancing. And the school required weekday chapel attendance and Sunday church attendance.

A somewhat difficult time for Peale came as he continued to struggle with reciting in class. A kind teacher, Professor Arneson, kept him after class one day and gave him two suggestions: 1) to ask Jesus to help him (with his inferiority complex), and 2) to look up the writings of American psychologist, William James. Norman followed through with his professor's advice and was greatly helped.

Some of Norman's professors, like his English professor, tended to emphasize the ideas and teaching of Ralph Waldo Emerson and psychologist William James, as well. Later on, Norman would incorporate some of their teachings into his theology and Sunday sermons.

Peale had already enrolled at Boston University following his undergraduate graduation. He signed up to get a master's degree in literature but also left room for theology classes. Before he completed his first year, however, he transferred to the Boston University School of Theology after receiving a "-call-" to the ministry.

By the time he graduated from theology school, Peale found himself in the midst of the "Roaring Twenties" with all the decade's optimism—despite prohibition being the law of the land. Much was changing in the country, including the role of religion in people's lives. The social gospel became more and more accepted, although Norman disdained it since he was a solid evangelical. He was called to his first church in Brooklyn, New York to King's Highway Methodist Church—with thirty thousand newcomers between 1921 and 1924.

Norman threw himself into his work. Being unmarried, he could donate his time to increasing church membership and building the church. His messages centered around having a friendly relationship with Jesus, although the services themselves were more formal with lofty, semi-classical music.

Then, in April, 1927, Norman was invited to preach at University Avenue Methodist Church in Syracuse, New York. Within the month, he was asked to become the church's new pastor. He titled his first sermon, "The Glory of the Future," using the tenth chapter of John's gospel as his text—He especially emphasized John 10:10: "The thief cometh not but for to steal, and to kill, and to destroy: but I am come that they might have life, and that they might have it more abundantly."

The church was located next to Syracuse University, a Methodist school with a few thousand students. Peale believed the established church had an important role to play in contemporary culture. In fact, he told his Syracuse congregation: "Only the Christian church can keep alive free institutions, the rights of man, and the sacredness of personality." (2)

Norman's overall message was still taking shape at this time. In a sermon at University Church near the end of the 1920's, he told his congregation about two "positive thinkers": One was the apostle Peter, and the other was arctic explorer Richard Byrd. He claimed the goals they achieved were provided by inner qualities available to everyone; in fact, he suggested heroic accomplishments came from "harmonizing life with the Spirit of Christ." (3) In addition, he confirmed, their achievements were not extraordinary, for "given a normal intelligence, an individual can make of himself about what he wants to do." [4]

Norman also called Jesus' Sermon on the Mount in Matthew's Gospel, a "practical program for personality building." (5) The majority of his sermons now focused on problems of daily living, although at this time the messages weren't concerned with technique. Membership at the church continued to grow during these years—even during the years of the stock market crash, membership mushroomed.

A newspaper reported of Peale at this time in the early 1930's that "he regularly preached to over a thousand at University Church and ventured that he was one of the most eloquent and attractive speakers in the state. He possessed an uncanny ability to understand the existential moment, to sense an audience and sculpt his message to its sensibilities; he had the intuitive skills of a populist, now honed by experience. Audiences didn't like him, they loved him." (6)

On June 20, 1930, Norman Vincent Peale and Ruth Stafford were married. The two seemed extraordinarily compatible and their marriage lasted over sixty years. Ruth had been a student at Syracuse University, and was eight years younger than Peale.

Then, in March, 1932, Norman received calls from two churches: First Methodist Church in Los Angeles, and Marble Collegiate in New York City. Although the California church had over seven thousand members, Marble Collegiate was better endowed as well as being an old, historic church. Finally, Peale decided on Marble Collegiate where he remained throughout his long ministry until he retired in 1984.

Some of the other endeavors of Peale were his writing career and his speaking career. Pastoring at Marble Collegiate gave him the freedom to pursue these activities. He instituted a "healing" clinic to encourage those individuals hit hard by the depression, Guideposts Magazine, the book, and *The Power of Positive Thinking,* which sold at least six million copies from its first publishing date in 1952. Probably Peale's advice to his constituents and many others to remain positive about their situation is good advice—advice that he himself followed despite some of life's seeming paradoxes along the way.

Here's what Peale had to say about prayer:

> "Faith begins as a thin trickle across the
> mind. Repeated, it becomes
> habitual. It cuts into the consciousness
> until, as you deepen the channel,
> faith-thought overflows and whatever you
> think about the world becomes
> optimistic and positive.

To be efficient in prayer you must learn
the art of praying. You can read
every book ever written about prayer,
and you can attend innumerable
discussions on prayer, but the only way to pray is to pray.
Make your prayers simple and natural...
talk to God as to a friend."

The Lord of Hosts is with you. Go, and conquer your land bearing fruit unto the glory of God (John 15:8). I'm sure the fruit is twofold: the fruit of the Spirit and fruit in the souls of men. You cannot lose with Jesus as your Leader and the Holy Spirit as your Guide and Comforter."

CHAPTER TWO

Declaring God's Word

"The prophet that hath a dream, let him tell a dream; and he that hath my word, let him speak my word faithfully. What is the chaff to the wheat? Is not my word like as a fire? Saith the Lord; and like a hammer that breaketh the rock in pieces?"
(Jeremiah 23: 28-29)

Jeremiah has been called the "Weeping Prophet" because of his sorrow and distress over his nation of Judah. Even though he prophesied during the reign of King Josiah, who was overall a righteous king, neither the king nor the nation knew what God's requirements were. In fact, the nation was very corrupt at this time.

Not until approximately 621 B.C., the Book of the Law was discovered in the temple by the priest Hilkiah. When the discovery occurred, King Josiah tore his clothes and set about initiating reforms concerning the Temple and worship of God in Judah. Sadly, a little later, the king, in an unwise gesture of reconciliation, joined forces with the northern kingdom of Israel and was killed in battle at Megiddo when the two armies of Judah and Israel fought against Pharaoh Necho of Egypt.

Although part of Jeremiah's message concerns judgment for Judah, in another part, he prophesied about the coming Messianic kingdom; Jeremiah accomplishes all this according to God's word which he confesses is like a fire and like a hammer that shatters the rock in pieces.

God's Word can accomplish many things in our lives. Even Joshua said in Joshua 1:8: "Do not let this book of the law depart from your mouth; meditate on it day and night, so that you may be careful to do everything written in it. Then you will be prosperous and successful." What a wonderful promise to the believer! God says as you "meditate" on his word day and night you will be prosperous and successful.

In Jeremiah 23:29, however, Jeremiah preaches to the Israelites who were worshipping the idols of Baal at this time. He urges them to repent and put away the idols from them. God's people were also disobedient by not keeping the law and were in moral decay. Jeremiah prophesies in earlier verses that the avengers from the north would come like a raging lion from the thicket. They would sweep over the land with chariots like the whirlwind and with horses swifter than eagles, and spread terror before them and leave ruin in their path (Jer. 4:13).

The good news in Jeremiah 23:29, however, is that God's word is like a fire. Fire destroys, but it also purges and cleanses. In 1980 at Mount St. Helens in Oregon, in the United States, for example, lava from the volcano burned and destroyed vegetation and everything in its path. Within a number of years, however, new growth appeared in the plants and grasses covering the mountain side. Similarly, in your life, God's word can cut you to the core of your being, then lift you back up and restore you to a higher level. Such actions by the Lord constitute His pruning, and if you obey, you'll come out stronger and wiser (John 15).

God's word is also like a hammer that breaks rock in pieces. The "rock" here refers to the human heart of stone before the word works on it. God's word can shatter a person's heart in many pieces—then put his heart back in a more subdued, humble way. In fact, God's word is so powerful, it "breaketh the cedars of Lebanon" and "the voice of the Lord divideth the flames of fire" (Psalm 29:5-7).

What are some of the hidden sins in your heart? Certainly pride is a chief sin. Because of Moses' sin of pride and killing the Egyptian as related by Stephen in Acts 7:24, the Lord had to send him to the back side of the desert for 40 years to humble him. Stephen also says in Acts 7:20 that "Moses was educated in all the wisdom of the Egyptians and was powerful in speech and action." How different Moses appeared after 40 years in the desert when he told God he "couldn't speak." The Lord had delivered him from self righteousness after his time in the desert. He had been "pruned" and chastened by God's word.

Andrew Carnegie, the self-taught steel magnate, promoted the Gospel by building and endowing public libraries all over America.

Carnegie's ancestral roots were in Dunfermline, Scotland, where he was born on November 25, 1835. His father, William, was a weaver, working his craft many hours a day on the first floor of the family home. His mother, Margaret Morrison Carnegie, helped her husband by keeping him supplied with spools of yarn that were constantly being unwound by the loom. In addition to helping her husband, Andrew's mother cooked, sewed, laundered, and managed the household. She also brought water from fountains, pumps, or wells, and gathered wood, charcoal, and coal from nearby sources.

Life was not easy for the Carnegies, although they were somewhat better off than the majority of their neighbors. Dunfermline had numerous cottages, all looking alike, built with gray stone and having two stories—like the Carnegie home. Situated in East-central Scotland, somewhat north of Edinburgh,

Scotland's capital, Dunfermline had a renowned history, In fact, many of the kings, queens, and princes of early Scotland were born, lived or were buried here.

Both of Andrew's parents were unusual in that they read newspapers and other materials to stay abreast of the political and current events of the day. His parents even broke away from the traditional church of the day, the Presbyterian, and embraced other faiths—his mother, the Unitarian, his father, Swedenborgianism.

By the time Andrew turned eight, two major changes occurred in his life: his brother, Thomas, was born, and the young boy realized his mother could no longer give him her full attention, so he started to school. Later, he claimed his parents waited until he wanted to go to school.

The school he went to was very formal, and the school master sat on a small raised platform at the front of the classroom. A leather strap lay beside him which he applied to any boy who misbehaved. But Andrew loved school and seldom had the strap applied to him.

Everything also changed for the Carnegie family when the looms in Scotland began to operate by steam. Andrew's father couldn't compete with the steam-powered looms and the family began a descent into poverty. Andrew's mother knew then it was time to emigrate to the United States.

When the Carnegies arrived in the United States, they went to Pittsburgh, Pennsylvania, located at the point where the Monongahela and Allegheny Rivers meet to form the Ohio River. Pittsburgh was little more than a frontier town in 1848. The Carnegies soon settled in with relatives already living in the area.

William Carnegie set up a loom to weave Homespun checkered tablecloths then popular, but he could not compete with the steam-powered looms in price and efficiency. So both father and son began working at a neighborhood mill, which was hard work, but at least they both had jobs.

Now Andrew began a rapid rise to success because of his diligent work habits and his intelligence. He left the factory job and became a "bobbin boy" at another location. A year later, he procured a job as a telegraph messenger boy at two and a half dollars a week-this was a 100% increase from where he started at his earlier job.

At his messenger boy job, Andrew didn't realize that being involved with the telegraph he was affiliated with the latest technology of the time. Nevertheless, he liked this job and later wrote, "From a dark cellar running a steam engine, begrimed with coal dirt and without a trace of the elevating traces of life, I was lifted into Paradise, yes, Heaven it seemed to me, with the newspapers, pens, pencils, and sunshine about me." (1)

Andy Carnegie soon became well known in downtown Pittsburgh as he memorized not only the street names and the city layout, but business people's names as well. And, as the new telegraph service flourished in Pittsburgh, so did Andy.

One day, the superintendent of the telegraph service visited the office, now consisting of five young men, all of Scottish descent. He saw the boys in rough street clothes and decided the company needed a better image, so he sent all of them to a tailor to be fitted with sharp, dark green uniforms.

While Andrew worked as a messenger boy, a Colonel James Anderson opened his library to working boys, and allowed them to check out one book a week. Andy never missed a week checking out books. In his spare time at the telegraph office, Andrew learned telegraphy, and a short time later, he became a telegraph operator, at seventeen, earning $25 a month.

He worked at the telegraph company as a clerk and telegrapher for the Pittsburgh division of the Pennsylvania Railroad. One day an accident occurred tying up the entire division while T.A. Scott, the division superintendent was out on the line and unreachable. Andy took matters into his own hands and kept things moving on the line by issuing orders and signing them, T.A. Scott. From that time on, Andy practically ran the entire division.

One day, Superintendent Scott asked him, "Andy, can you find $500 to invest?" (2)

Truthfully, about all young Carnegie had was 500 cents, but he asked for more information. Scott told him about a station agent who wanted to sell ten shares of Adams Express for $500. Scott said it was a good opportunity.

Andrew talked things over with his resourceful mother that evening, and she decided to borrow $500 from a relative using the house as collateral. A month later, Andrew received an envelope addressed to Andrew Carnegie, Esquire that contained a dividend check for $10. Andrew was thrilled with the idea of investing money, not working for it, and receiving the reward from it.

Soon, another opportunity came to Andrew. A man came to him asking his opinion about a "sleeping car" idea he had. The man was T.T. Woodruff, inventor of the railroad sleeping car.

Success followed success for Carnegie, and before long he invested in the oil fields of Pennsylvania. Then he realized in 1864, that the country's railroads needed much repair, so he began to manufacture iron rails. In addition, he formed the Keystone Bridge Company, calling for the construction of iron railroad bridges to span the rivers.

Carnegie, a small man, only five feet, four inches tall, had a genius for handling situations and men. He soon met with George Pullman to consolidate their rival sleeping car companies. Before long, the Pullman Palace Car Company had a worldwide monopoly on sleeping cars.

Carnegie next invested in an oil field in Pennsylvania. He invested during the time of the Civil War in the United States, and no one could foresee the use of oil at that time. But he took a risk in his investment, not the first, nor the last. Carnegie always seemed to be in the right place at the right time to get in on a profitable venture.

Now, in 1866, Carnegie decided to put his businesses on hold and take an extended European trip. He and two friends sailed for Europe visiting all the great cities like Amsterdam, London, Paris, and Berlin. So for nine months they traveled by train, ship and horse-drawn carriages.

Upon his return to the United States, in late 1866, Carnegie plunged back into his work. In each of his investments, he tried to keep in touch with the company and not let it exist without his input. He also knew he needed more capital to manage his investments. He realized, too, that he needed to go to New York City to find the needed finances. So, in 1867, Andy moved to New York City, along with his mother. The Carnegies rented rooms in what was the finest hotel in America, the St. Nicholas Hotel in lower Manhattan.

New York City seemed to be waiting for Andrew Carnegie. He already had a good reputation in a few business circles, and he set about widening those circles. He was known for his boundless energy, good humor, plain speech, honesty and his genius for dealing with all types of people. Hi connection with the British also helped him gain the confidence of investors.

By 1874, following the financial panic of the previous year, Carnegie bought out his competition in the steel business. At that time he dominated the steel business until Charles Schwab, Elbert H. Gary, and J. Pierpont Morgan discussed a plan for a billion-dollar company to dominate the steel business of the world. They asked Carnegie if he would sell his business; he said, "Yes," and named his price. Although they fumed about it, they finally gave in to Carnegie, who received $490,000,000 in bonds, preferred stock, and in common stock.

After completing the deal, Carnegie announced to the world that he considered it a disgrace to die rich and didn't intend to be disgraced. Thus, he donated $a $5,000,000 fund to the men of his mills; he started library gifts with five and a quarter million dollars for sixty-eight branch libraries in New York City; he gave $28,000,000 to the Carnegie Institute in Pittsburgh; $25,000,000 to the Carnegie Institute in Washington, D.C., organized to assist any activity for the Carnegie Hero Fund, and gave additional monies away for worthy causes. When Carnegie died in 1919, he had given away over $300,000,000. He was left with a modest estate of $30,000,000. But in addition, many small towns across the U.S. benefitted from Carnegie libraries—the remarkable legacy of a remarkable man who rediscovered himself in a new world.

So, too, in your life, the Word of God, as Jeremiah declares, will prune and chasten you as you study it. What a marvelous privilege you have—to meditate on God's Word and to grow spiritually. You can not only help yourself through this process, but you also help others.

CHAPTER THREE

Bearing Witness

**"You will be his witness to all men
of what you have seen and heard.
And now what are you waiting for? Get
up, and be baptized and wash your sins away,
calling on his name" (Acts 22:14-15, NIV).**

Some of the ways you can bear witness for the Lord are through your attitudes, your words, and your deeds, or actions. The book of Acts, although displaying the forming and actions of the early church, has also been referred to as "the acts of the Holy Spirit." The book begins with the coming of the Holy Spirit in the second chapter of Acts—like a "mighty wind" and with "flames of fire" on each person's head.

Here's the account in Acts 2: 2-3, NIV: "When the day of Pentecost came, they were all together in one place. Suddenly a sound like the blowing of a violent wind came from heaven and filled the whole house where they were sitting. They saw what seemed to be tongues of fire that separated and came to rest on each of them."

Once a person is born again, God wants to use them to be a witness to the Resurrection of Jesus Christ. The believer then needs to point out to the unbeliever what it means to him to have Christ living inside of him. He tells him about the peace and joy Christ brings once he enters a person's heart. The peace and joy come as a result of knowing his sins are forgiven and he has "peace with God."

What good news this is! As a believer, you should want to shout it from the mountain tops. You also have eternal life in Jesus Christ.

So, what are some of the ways you can bear witness to Christ? First of all, you can show that you have Christ in you through your attitude. Jack, for example has known the Lord for around a year. He had been addicted to drugs, but the Lord not only saved him but set him free from his drug habit. He delights now in telling others what Christ has done for him and leads many to Christ. Jack isn't perfect, but he realizes that the Holy Spirit is working in him and is sanctifying him as he reads the Bible daily.

Bob, on the other hand, has been a Christian for at least ten years. While he knows he's a believer, he struggles with getting angry and losing his temper. He does share his faith on occasion, but sometimes his bad temper destroys his witness. The Lord can help him overcome his bad temper, and hopefully, he will learn to overcome it. As the Apostle Paul says in Ephesians 4:17-18: "That you must no longer live as the Gentiles do….They are darkened in their understanding and separated from the life of God…due to the hardening of their hearts."

Paul adds, "In your anger, do not sin…and do not give the devil a foothold" (Eph. 4:27, NIV). Besides sharing verbally, you can also witness through your actions and deeds reaching out to others as you have opportunity. James points out in his epistle: "What good is it if a man claims to have faith but has no deeds….Suppose a brother or sister is without clothes and daily food. Although you may wish them well, that's not the Christ-like thing to do. The Christian needs to reach out with proper clothing and nourishing food. Or, at least point the way to a shelter or place where their needs can be met.

Cyrus McCormick, the man who invented the reaper, illustrates how inventive genius can bear witness.

Sweat poured off the body of fifteen-year-old Cyrus McCormick as he rhythmically cut the wheat in his father's fields with a curve-handled scythe. The sun was hot and Cyrus wanted to rest, but he still had another one to two acres to cut before the day was over. He thought to himself, "There must be a way to use horses to cut and harvest wheat." (1)

As he experimented with various tools in his father's log blacksmith shop later on in the evening, the thought came back of designing a reaper that used horses instead of human labor. His father had already designed a number of farm inventions but a workable reaper eluded him.

Cyrus Hall McCormick was born on his father's farm on February 15, 1809. Cyrus was the first child of Robert and Mary Ann or "Polly" McCormick. Walnut Grove, the McCormick Farm, was located in Rockbridge County, Virginia. Later on, as he prospered, Robert owned 1200 acres of fertile farm land. The nearest town, Staunton, was eighteen miles north of the farm. The Atlantic Ocean lay 100 miles due east.

In addition to farming, Robert also owned two grist mills, two saw mills, a smelting furnace, a distillery, and a blacksmith shop. Robert was a talented inventor as well with an unusual aptitude in mechanics. He invented new types of farm machinery: a hemp brake, a clover huller, a bellows, and a threshing machine. Only twenty-four feet square with an uneven floor, the blacksmith shop had a forge on each side of the chimney enabling two men to work hot metal at the same time.

Cyrus later wrote, "My father was both mechanical and inventive, and could and did at that time use the tools of his shop in making any piece of machinery he wanted. He invented, made, and patented several more or less valuable agricultural implements...but most of his inventions dropped into disuse after the lapse of some years." (2)

When Cyrus was five years old, he came down with yellow fever. Both his mother's parents and brother had already died from the deadly disease. The doctor left a "lancet" at the McCormick home telling Robert to "bleed" his young son. Robert, however, refused; instead, he immersed the boy in hot baths containing bitter herbs and whiskey and giving him hot tea to drink. He completely recovered a short time later.

Prior to adolescence, at around the age of eight, Cyrus attended Old Field School not far from the McCormick farm; his mother and father also taught him at home. He received daily instruction in Scripture, catechism, and other spiritual studies from his Scotch-Irish Presbyterian parents. His father also taught him to use the tools in his blacksmith shop as well as involving him in business operations. Some of Cyrus' schoolbooks were Murray's Grammar, Dilworth's Arithmetic, Webster's Spelling Book, Adam's Geography, and the New York Primer.

As he grew to adolescence, Cyrus was six feet, two inches tall, with a muscular build, but having small hands and feet. At this time, the young man gave more attention to devising a reaping machine that worked. To do so, he needed to overcome the problems his father encountered: the machine needed to cut the ripe grain, but also handle and deliver the cut grain.

Cyrus' first success with a reaper prototype came in July, 1831. The machine was pulled by a single horse, guided by a rider. The horse walked through previously cut stubble before the right side of a cross-wise-extending cutter bar with an associated reciprocating blade, which the horse drew; it cut a swath through ripe grain on the left side.

As the cutter bar advanced and the grain cut, the grain moved back and fell upon a horizontal platform trailing behind the cutter bar. The cut grain was raked by hand off the platform to the open (right) or stubble side (behind the horse) by a raker who walked alongside the machine.

Cyrus' bigger job now was to convince farmers for the need of his new machine. He continued to make improvements on it even at a time when other people were also inventing reapers and getting patents on them. However, McCormick's design was superior to the others.

Riding his horse home one day, the thought came to Cyrus, "Perhaps I may make a million dollars from this reaper." (3) He said in later years, "This thought was so enormous that it seemed like a dream—like dwelling in the clouds—so remote, so unattainable, so exalted, so visionary." (4)

Cyrus decided at that point to create a business from his reaper. He couldn't be content building a few reapers in his father's blacksmith's shop. He started to advertise his reaper; although this was unheard of in the 1830's. In the meantime, Cyrus paid thirty dollars to the U.S. Treasury and on June 21, 1834, obtained a patent on his reaper.

McCormick was not alone in his invention. In fact, roughly one hundred other individuals had also invented some type of reaper. A serious competitor, Obed Hussey, posed a dire threat to McCormick's number one position. As it turned out, after several side-by-side trials of the two reapers, Cyrus's reaper always operated more efficiently. After while, Hussey was past history.

McCormick's problem now was to locate a more convenient manufacturing location. Virginia, and anywhere on the East Coast was too far away from the "Great Plains" area of the country. The inventor finally settled on Chicago as the best location to produce his machine.

In addition to finding a suitable location, McCormick still had to overcome the farmers' skepticism. To overcome this last obstacle, McCormick devised a credit plan whereby a farmer could put so much toward the Reaper's purchase, then pay the rest after harvest. After solving a number of problems with his new plan, it proved to be a turning point for producing and selling the Reaper.

In 1846, Cyrus began to enjoy success with his Reaper. As H.E. Towner of Will County, Illinois, said in July 1846, "I consider it [the McCormick Reaper] to the western country the most important invention of the age, and that it will greatly increase the product of the country, not being able without it to reap so much as can be sown." (5)

More praise and endorsement came from the editor of the Chicago Daily Journal, who said the McCormick Reaper "Will cut from 15 to 20 acres per day, which is as decided an advantage as the Magnetic Telegraph is on steam. These machines are highly useful in this state, where the harvest is large, while the means of saving it is disproportionately small." (6)

Later on, McCormick also sold reapers in Europe with some success. England and France even decorated him for his invention. From the beginning of his business of manufacturing the reaper, he had various problems: with defective reapers, inadequate business partners, etc., but his tough Scotch-Irish ancestry served him well. He was a stern, self-disciplined man who always refused to take the easy way out. As he persevered in business and solved his problems, his business prospered, and he became very wealthy. Toward the end of his life, he contributed to a Presbyterian Seminary in Chicago (now called McCormick Seminary), and endowed a chair in Washington and Lee University in Virginia.

All the way along his amazing journey to power and wealth, McCormick was forced to change the way he thought about doing things—his "fixed" habits. He had to continually solve the problems caused by manufacturing and distribution. In his lifetime, he manufactured more than six million reapers continually making improvement on his original reaper. The dream he had earlier about becoming wealthy and successful had come true.

Many ways exist for a believer to share their faith. The Holy Spirit in each Christian will guide them to people who need Christ and will even give them the words to say.

What a joy and privilege it is to share the "Good News" of Christ. The more you share, the better and easier it gets. As Christians, we are the Lord's witnesses.

CHAPTER FOUR

Walking in Integrity

"The integrity of the upright shall guide them, but the perverseness of transgressors shall destroy them." (Proverbs 11:3, KJV)

This verse is found in the Book of Proverbs—a practical book of wisdom largely compiled by King Solomon—the wisest man who ever lived. God visited Solomon as a young man after his father, King David, died. The Lord said He would give Solomon the desires of his heart, whatever they were. So, Solomon asked for wisdom to guide his people. His request pleased the Lord, and He added riches and honor to Solomon's request.

In Proverbs 11:3, the believer is urged to walk in "Integrity." The only way a believer can walk in integrity and faithfulness is to study the Bible daily, pray and listen to the Holy Spirit for guidance.

Integrity means "Steadfast adherence to a strict moral or ethical code." In other words, to have integrity is to walk honestly, seeking God's kingdom first, keeping your word with people and walking circumspectly. In Matthew 6:33, the Bible says to "Seek ye first the kingdom of God and his righteousness; and all these things {material possessions, etc.}shall be added unto you."

What does it mean to seek God's kingdom first? I believe it means to put God first throughout the day. When you get up in the morning, for example, maybe even before you eat breakfast, reach for your Bible and begin to study it. You might read one or two chapters in the Old and New Testaments, Psalms and Proverbs. I like to use the "One-year Bible" daily reading plan which takes you through the Bible in a year. The main idea, though, is to read, or "meditate" until the Holy Spirit speaks to you. Whatever the Spirit says to you is your "manna" for the day. You need to keep a favorite scripture in mind: "Man shall not live by bread alone, but by every word that proceeds from the mouth of God" (Matt. 4:7, KJV).

William Tyndale (1490-1536), the English Reformer and Translator of the English Bible, made it his life's goal to translate the Bible into English. He said (paraphrasing), "A man though he drives the plow shall be able to understand the Scriptures." Tyndale was burned at the stake in Holland by King Henry VIII's assailants in 1536 after translating the New Testament and sections of the Old Testament into English. The later King James Version of the Bible was largely the work of William Tyndale.

A second aspect of Integrity is to keep your word. Abraham Lincoln, also known as "Honest Abe," is reputed to have walked miles to return a penny given to him in error. Even in daily life, if a clerk refunds too much money to you in change, you can always politely tell him that the change is too much and give the extra money back. Or, if you have an item due someone and you miss the deadline, try to communicate with that person and work out the situation. The Lord sees and hears your conversation. He will forgive you if you sincerely repent and ask forgiveness for your shortcomings. But perhaps you need to plan better to avoid not being able to keep your word.

Last of all, the Bible talks about walking circumspectly. As Ephesians 5:15-19, NIV, says, "Be very careful then, how you live—not as unwise but as wise, making the most of every opportunity because the days are evil. Therefore do not be foolish but understand what the Lord's will is." The apostle Paul then reminds the believer not to be drunk with wine but be filled with the Spirit—and also to speak to one another in Psalms, hymns and spiritual songs." The apostle adds, for you to always be thankful. If you believe (as the Bible teaches in 1 Thess. 5:18): "In everything give thanks: for this is the will of God in Christ Jesus concerning you."

Abraham Lincoln, the sixteenth president of the United States and President during the Civil War, was a man who walked in integrity. In the midst of the War, he made the statement, "I claim not to have controlled events but confess plainly that events have controlled me." (1)

Lincoln, a self-made man, made the most of a difficult situation. Born in a log cabin in Hodgenville, Kentucky on February 12, 1809, Abe's early life consisted of farming, manual labor, and splitting rails. Abe's father grew up as an orphan from the time he was six when Indians killed his father while he worked in the fields. The name "Abraham," Thomas's father's name was long—like the young Abraham Lincoln who stood six feet at the age of twelve.

When Abraham turned seven, the family moved from Kentucky to Indiana where Thomas saw greater opportunity to obtain good land. Here where the wilderness came nearly to the front door, the Lincolns hewed out lumber from the trees to make a cabin. They carved out more lumber for making tables and benches to use inside.

Some time later, Abraham's mother died following a brief illness. The young boy, his older sister, Sarah, and his father were much saddened by her death. The children's cousin, Dennis, also bereft of Abraham's aunt and uncle who died from drinking "tainted milk" caused by a cow eating poisonous plants, moved in with them. Twelve-year-old Sarah tried to fill her mother's role in cooking and cleaning, but often despaired from weariness.

Over a year later, the family was cheered when Sarah Bush Johnston, a widow with three children, agreed to marry Thomas Lincoln. When Sarah arrived in the Lincoln home, she worked hard and scrubbed the children clean. She even had Thomas cut a hole in the cabin for a window, covering it with greased paper, a substitute for glass at the time. She also had Thomas build an attic room where the three boys could sleep. Sarah loved her new step son calling him "The best boy I ever saw or ever expect to see." (3) Abraham even called her "Mama," as she replaced his own mother in his heart.

Sarah Lincoln also encouraged Abraham to attend school, despite the fact that his father thought it unnecessary. Abraham rushed home after school to catch up on chores. Every chance Abe got, though, he read—even in the field at each opportunity. While not many books were available, his stepmother brought a number of them with her from Kentucky. The young boy read the family Bible as well as *The Pilgrim's Progress* and *Aesop's Fables*. His favorite book, though, was *The Life of George Washington*. He liked the book's accounts of the battlefields and the country's struggles for liberty.

His stepmother noted about him, "When he came across a passage that struck him, he would write it down on boards." (4) When the board was used up, he whittled it down for more use. He practiced over and over and became so good at spelling and writing that illiterate neighbors called on him to compose their letters for them.

Abraham's innate melancholy disposition was tempered by a fun-loving spirit. He even played the part of a ham at times—especially when he mounted a tree stump to imitate local politicians.

At age twenty-one, in the early spring of 1830, Abraham's family moved near Decatur, Illinois to find better farm land. Many settlers moved to Illinois at the same time clearing the land of its abundant trees and forests. The wood from the trees furnished lumber for homes, fences, and heating. Some of the challenges the Lincoln family faced during their move were frozen ground just beginning to thaw under a faint spring sun; melting snow flooding the rivers and covering the roads, making the roads muddy, and difficult for the oxen to pull their loads; crossing frozen streams, or wading through icy-cold water since there were no bridges. When crossing one frozen river, Abraham's pet dog fell through the ice, so Abraham jumped from the wagon and waded into the waist-high water, and pulled his pet to safety.

In the summer and fall, Abraham and his cousin plowed the land (after first building a cabin), and raised a crop of corn. They also built a split-rail fence around ten acres, enclosing the land and the cabin. Unfortunately, the family's troubles worsened in the autumn when they all came down with malaria and fever. During the winter of 1830, deep snow fell for two months and snow drifts covered the cabin. Then an icy rain fell covering the snow drifts while temperatures plummeted to zero and stayed there for two months.

Since people stayed in their cabins, cattle froze to death and even wild animals starved to death. With the coming of spring when the snow melted, it flooded the rivers and countryside. In addition, there was little game to hunt. Then cholera struck, killing thousands of people. At last the nightmare subsided. But Abraham felt restless. When a local trader, Dennis Offutt, gave Lincoln and his cousin a chance to take goods on a flat boat to New Orleans, Lincoln jumped at the chance. The trip opened a whole new world to him as he observed slaves being bought and sold and working in the fields.

Abraham ended up spending a month in New Orleans before returning home. When he was ready, he booked passage on a steamboat headed for St. Louis; from there, he walked across Illinois to his father's cabin. The man who employed him to take the flatboat to New Orleans now hired him for his general store, plus he could sleep in the back. His employer, Denton Offutt, was very pleased with Abraham, telling everyone how smart and strong he was. Although the average height for a man at this time was five feet six inches, Abraham's height was now six feet four inches.

He was content with his position at the General Store, but not satisfied. Sometime later, Abraham's neighbors asked him to draft deeds and other legal papers for them. Doing these chores plus the local judges asking him to comment on various court cases, led the young man to believe he could run for political office. He lost the election and a short time later, lost his job at the General Store.

Then, he was asked to be the postmaster in New Salem, Illinois. As postmaster, he could read all the papers that arrived in addition to talking with the customers. While at the post office, Lincoln received the opportunity to be a surveyor. He enlisted the aid of the schoolmaster to help him learn geometry and trigonometry—tools he needed as a surveyor. When he mastered these skills, he set off as a surveyor to plan routes for roads, boundaries and farms. He also met many of the people who later voted for him in the next campaign. He won the next election in 1834 and was elected to the Illinois House of Representatives. He knew he needed to learn the law to do a good job as a state legislator, which he set out to do.

After Lincoln studied for years on his own, he became a lawyer in 1837, and a friend, John Todd Stuart offered him a position in his busy Springfield law office. During that time, too, Lincoln courted Mary Todd, "The belle of Springfield," and married her in 1843. He also formed a new law partnership with William Herndon, who joined Lincoln's firm as a junior partner. Even though others who saw Lincoln's office called it "a mess," the disorder suited the partners who could usually find what they needed—even in Lincoln's stove pipe hat! Herndon referred to Lincoln's hat as "an extraordinary receptacle, his desk and memorandum book." (5)

One of his duties every spring and fall was to ride "the circuit" with a judge. The two traveled from one county seat to another holding court and staying at crowded inns. Sometimes as many as twenty men shared a room, some sleeping on quilts spread on the floor. Through these experiences, Lincoln got to know many people who voted him into office at a later date.

Following a series of debates with Stephen Douglas in 1858, Lincoln lost a bid for the Senate. Although he did his best in the debates, he believed he would be forgotten afterward. Instead, the debates with Douglas had brought him national fame and he received numerous invitations to speak. All his speeches paved the way for his presidential election in 1860.

Abraham Lincoln, a self-educated man who suffered many hardships early in his life, always retained a sense of humor. However, he was adamant about slavery and tried to have it outlawed in the District of Columbia after he was elected to the U.S. Senate in 1848, and the Lincoln family moved to Washington, D.C. Lincoln believed slavery was an evil thing in the capital of a country dedicated to liberty.

Lincoln was first elected as President of the United States in 1860, and in January 1863, he signed the "Emancipation Proclamation," announcing the freeing of all slaves then in arms against the United States. Much debate had taken place in the halls of Congress over the issue of slavery, and as each new state came into the Union, a determination had to be made: would it be slave or free?

The U.S. Civil War (the War Between the States) started in April, 1861, and began over the issue of slavery—or "States' Rights." The Southern states wanted to retain slavery since almost their entire economy was based on agriculture, and slaves were needed to work the land. Lincoln had his hands full after the war began. He faced various crises including finding good, competent generals and the depletion of the national treasury. The president met each one with a studied coolness and usually came up with the correct response.

By the time of the next presidential election in 1864, Lincoln was voted in unanimously. He still had his hands very full, although the war was winding down. Then on April 9, 1865, General Robert E. Lee, general of the Confederate forces, surrendered at Appomattox Courthouse in Appomattox, Virginia. The terrible war was over. Less than a week later, when Abraham and Mary Lincoln attended a play at Ford's theatre in Washington, a deranged actor, John Wilkes Booth, shot and killed the president, although he lingered for another day or so.

During his tenure as president, Lincoln sought guidance from God continually. He remarked on one occasion, "I have been driven many times to my knees by the overwhelming conviction that I had nowhere else to go." Surely the guidance he received from the Almighty brought the president and the country safely through the War and preserved the Union.

The Lord is not a hard taskmaster, but He does want His children to walk and live in integrity and obedience. With the Holy Spirit living inside you, you can enjoy a happy, fruitful life in Christ. Decide today to do just that.

CHAPTER FIVE

Helping Others

**"Dear Friend, you are faithful in what
you are doing for the brothers, even though they
are strangers to you. They have told the church
about your love. You will do well to send
them on their way in a manner worthy of God."
(3 John 1:5, NIV)**

Whatever you do for the Lord, it always comes back to you many fold. As Psalm 37:4 says, "Delight thyself in the Lord; and he shall give you the desires of your heart."

A well-known English preacher and poet said it this way: "No man is an island, entire of itself; every man is a piece of the continent, a part of the main" (John Donne {1572-1631}. Since we're all interconnected, especially as Christians, it is our responsibility to reach out to one another in love and fellowship.

One of the obvious ways you can help another person is to offer hospitality. Even the apostle Peter, in Acts 10:23, invited the servants of Cornelius to spend the night at his home. The next day, he accompanied them to Cornelius' place where he shared the "Good News" of Christ with them. Part of being hospitable is to be friendly and solicitous toward others' welfare.

Not only should you be hospitable toward others in your own home, but exercise the gift of hospitality towards people you meet every day. People today tend to hide behind answering machines and other devices. Sometimes, it's difficult to hear a cheerful voice on the telephone. Everyone has problems and difficulties in life, but a happy smile, a cheerful voice can alleviate another's problems. Hospitality is an art: learn to practice it.

Another aspect of helping others is giving. Of course, you can give in different ways, but the Bible says much about giving: "Give and it shall be given unto you; good measure, pressed down, and shaken together, and running over, shall men give unto your bosom. For with the same measure that you mete withal it shall be measured to you again" (Luke 6:38, KJV). First of all, you should give to the Lord in tithes and offerings; but also as you see others in need, reach out to them with a financial gift—even a five or ten-dollar bill will be a blessing to them.

When the wife of a friend of mine was giving birth, I sent him a fifty-dollar cheque—even though I didn't have much money at the time. The money blessed him greatly, and I felt good about it. It is truly more blessed to give than to receive. You can give in other ways, too. Maybe an article of clothing, like a jacket, would keep someone warm in chilly weather. Look through your closet and pick out clothing you no longer use, and give it to someone who can use it. Sometimes, if you contact a charitable organization, they will come and pick up various articles you don't need.

Finally, you can help others by just giving them a helping hand. In the early days of the U.S. and Canada, when people were settling in the Western areas of the countries, neighbors would help each other with barn-raising and cabin-building. These projects drew neighbors closer together as they helped each other with their building projects.

In the Bible, too, you see in the story of the good Samaritan, the love of Christ working through the Samaritan toward the injured man. Several other individuals, including a priest and a Levite, couldn't risk becoming "unclean" according to the law. But the passage in Luke says when the Samaritan came to where the wounded man was, "he had compassion on him….bound up his wounds," put him on his own beast and brought him to an inn where he paid for his keep.

Dale Carnegie, author of the well-known book, *How to Win Friends and Influence People,* provides a wonderful example of helping others. He struggled early on to be a success in life. Carnegie became famous for his book, yet in his own speaking, he seemed rambling and incoherent, and his Midwestern twang added little to his delivery. Even when his book was the number one best seller, he experienced astonishment at his fame. In the course of his career, Dale found himself branded as "cynical, conniving, and manipulative." (1)

Who was this paradoxical person? Born November 24, 1888, Dale Carnegie grew up on a small, impoverished farm in Northwest Missouri near the "102" River. Yearly, the river flooded the fertile farmland at harvest time wiping out what might have been a bountiful harvest of corn, and drenched the hay. In addition, "Season after season, the fat hogs sickened and died from cholera, the bottom fell out of the market for cattle and mules, and the bank threatened to foreclose the mortgage." (2)

Dale's early family life revolved around the farm, home, and Harmony Methodist Church. The family moved numerous times in Dale's early years, finally settling on a farm in 1904 near Warrensburg, Missouri, about fifty miles south of Kansas City, Missouri. The family made their final move so Dale could attend Warrensburg State Teachers College and not have to board. Students preparing to teach could attend tuition free so that's what Dale did, riding his horse back and forth over the three miles each day.

Conscious of his tattered, patched clothing in college, Dale struggled to excel at something. He was a mediocre student, not because he lacked the drive to excel, however, but because of the hardness of his life. His father told him about a difficult time in his own life when the family still lived on the Maryville farm in 1898. Dale's father had been turned down for a loan request by a Maryville banker who had threatened to foreclose on the farm. On the way home he crossed the bridge over the 102 River. The accumulation of debts, the incessant toil, discouragement, and worry fastened on him in an unrelenting grip. He stopped the buggy, gazed at the tumultuous current, contemplated leaping in and ending it all. Dale's father told him later, "If it had not been for mother's religious faith, he would not have had the courage to live through those terrible years." (3)

Another chore Dale remembered doing when he was growing up was taking care of new-born piglets. He says of that responsibility (usually in February): "The last thing I did before I went to bed at night was to take that basket of pigs from behind the kitchen stove out to the hog shed, wait for them to nurse, and then bring them back and put them behind the stove." (4) The whole process was repeated a few hours later after which he got up to study his Latin verbs.

In college, Dale had had some success in speaking and debating. He realized he could win approval by applying these skills, so that's what he tried to do after leaving college. He tried sales and a few other jobs, and though he did well, the jobs had draw backs, too. Finally, Dale headed to New York seeking to fulfill a desire to get into show business.

When he reached New York City, miraculously, the American Academy of Dramatic Arts accepted Dale as a student. The Academy emphasized being natural and sincere as actors. Edward G. Robinson was a fellow student with Carnegie and left the school to succeed in Hollywood later on. The Academy's director,

Charles Jehlinger, had issued the following statement regarding the school's principles (two years before Carnegie entered the school): "To create an accent on naturalism accompanied by emotional recall in order to achieve a deeper, more essential 'truth' in performance." (5) The statement of purpose is close to what Carnegie would teach in public speaking later in his own courses.

After a brief acting debut with a travelling actor's group, Dale needed to find a way to earn a living. So he approached the program director of the 125th Street YMCA in New York City. The "Y" already advertised a "Harlem Evening School" and Dale thought he could teach Public Speaking in an evening class. The director said he could present his ideas at a social evening. When Dale's turn came, he recited a poem by James Whitcomb Riley called "Knee Deep in June." The recitation met with applause and Dale was hired to teach a night session of public speaking at $2 per session.

The first session, however, was nearly the last. Dale looked at a sea of blank faces and knew he was in trouble. The tutoring techniques he practiced in college weren't working with these businessmen. He called on a man in the back row to talk about himself. Before long, the class "took off." The key was getting class members on their feet talking about topics they knew— usually about themselves. Three seasons later, Dale earned $30 a night in commissions.

The course continued to grow and evolve as Dale improvised on the classes. With the publication of his book, *How to Win Friends and Influence People* in 1936, Dale's income was assured. Because of the book, people now came to Carnegie wondering where they could take the course. Many well-known people signed up for Carnegie's courses, including Lee Iacocca and Lowell Thomas, who became a life-long friend. Today, the book has gone through hundreds of editions and countless revisions and updates. Lowell Thomas endorsed the Carnegie Course, calling it, "Unique, a combination of public speaking, human relations and applied psychology."(6) At last, Dale Carnegie had achieved a greater success than he ever dreamed—far away from the 102 River and Warrensburg State Teachers College in Missouri—all because he used the skills he already had, and built an amazing course from them. He enabled millions of people all over the world to become more effective in their lives than they ever dreamed possible.

Jesus concludes the episode of the "Good Samaritan" by asking which of these three, was a good neighbor? In your daily life, as Jesus says here, you are to show mercy to those around you. So, if you are to help others, you need to be led by the Holy Spirit as to what to do and to whom to offer help. You can take comfort in knowing the Holy Spirit will never mislead you.

CHAPTER SIX

Doing Work

**"But as for you, be strong and do
not give up, for your work will be
rewarded"
(2 Chronicles 15:7)**

In his wisdom, God created each person for a specific purpose, or work. No two of us are alike. Even identical twins have subtle differences: like a mole in an unusual place or a different cast of eyes. The twins can tell you right away how they are "different."

Many places in the Bible also advise us to work diligently, and not be lazy. Nehemiah provides an example for us. Nehemiah was the cup bearer at the court of King Artaxerxes in Persia, which was a high honor. But in this position, Nehemiah had not forgotten his people, the Jews. God had promised to bring the Jews back to Jerusalem after 70 years in Babylon (Jeremiah 25-29). As Nehemiah asked some visiting Jews about the progress on the temple walls, he learned of the sad state of everything there. The news saddened him and he asked the king for permission to return to Jerusalem to work on the walls, and the King granted his request.

When Nehemiah reached Jerusalem in 445 BC, Ezra the priest had already been in Jerusalem 13 years. He had taught the people the Word of God, but Nehemiah was a civil engineer and could organize the rebuilding of the wall. Shortly after he arrived in the city, he went up and viewed the walls at night. When he saw their dilapidated condition, he urged the people to start building immediately, and the people were eager to do so "for the people had a mind to work" (Nehemiah 4:6).

After that, Nehemiah organized his "rebuilding committee" by families and other groups, each with their own portion of the wall to work on. One of the important things to remember when the Lord calls you to do something is to be prompt and not to be lazy, or procrastinate. Here, in this example from Nehemiah, the people started to work immediately. Because of their diligence, the wall was rebuilt within a reasonably short time.

A Christian should also be industrious and persistent in whatever God has called him to do. If you have difficulty getting started in your work, ask the Lord to help you. You also need to bind the devil off all hindrances to your work. The Lord wants to help you—and He wants to help you do a good job.

Even Nehemiah's workers experienced opposition from Sanballat and Tobiah and others, like the Ammonites and the Ashdodites. It's important for you to remember that you will face satanic opposition, too. You will need to do what Nehemiah's workers did: the people prayed, but also took up weapons while they worked: "From that day on, half of my men did the work, while the other half were equipped with spears, shields, bows and armor...Those who carried materials did their work with one hand and held a weapon in the other, and each of the builders wore his sword at his side as he worked" (Nehemiah 4:16-18).

Today, as New Testament believers, the apostle Paul tells us in Ephesians six: "For our struggle is not against flesh and blood, but against the rulers...authorities, against the powers of this dark work and against the spiritual forces of evil in the heavenly realms." This New Testament scripture is powerful because it spells out for the believer that he has a very real enemy in this world.

Your life as a Christian is not all "peaches and cream." God has work for you to do and you have a real enemy (Satan) who tries to stop you from doing your work. Last of all, be thorough in the work God calls you to do. The old saying, "If it's worth doing, it's worth doing right" still applies today, especially for the Christian. In Colossians, Paul urges the people "And whatsoever ye do, do it heartily, as to the Lord, and not unto men" (Col. 3:23). Whatever work you do, perform it as unto the Lord, not haphazardly, or without thought but put your whole heart into it. The Lord sees everything and He will reward you.

Clara Barton, a Civil War Nurse and Founder of the American Red Cross proved to be an amazing woman. Small of stature and patriotic from an early age, Clarissa Harlowe Barton (Clara) was born on December 25, 1821, in North Oxford, Massachusetts. Her parents, Stephen Barton and Sarah Stone Barton, already had four children: Dorothy (Dolly), age 17, Stephen, age 15, David, age 13, and Sally, age 10.

From a young child, Clara enjoyed sitting on her "soldier father's" lap listening to his stories of war. Through these stories she learned much about military strategy and tactics. Her father, a successful farmer, horse breeder, and local politician, sometimes moderated town meetings. He gave money regularly to help the poor, and even used his own money to establish a home for the poor. Earlier in his life he had been a soldier and fought against American Indians with future U.S. President William Henry Harrison. He was present during the war of 1812 when the great Shawnee leader, Tecumseh, was killed.

Because of her father's influence, Clara said, "I early learned that next to Heaven, our highest duty was to love and serve our country, and honor and support its laws." (1) On the other hand, Clara's mother taught the young girl many useful household skills like sewing, cooking, gardening, weaving cloth, canning fruit, and milking cows. Clara's mother, a plain hard-working woman, saw no need for her daughter to have dolls, or toys. Instead, Clara worked alongside her sisters doing household chores and learned not to complain or fuss.

Clara also learned many useful things from her siblings. Her sister, Dolly, already a teacher when Clara was born, helped care for her little sister. Her brother, Stephen, too, was already a teacher at the time of her birth, but took over his father's textile mill a few years later. Stephen, a gifted mathematician, taught Clara arithmetic on her little slate.

Even her older brother, David, contributed to her education. David loved animals and the outdoors. He was patient with his little sister and taught her to pound a nail with a hammer and throw a ball like a boy. One of the important things David taught Clara, however, was to ride horses bareback. Clara learned, at five years of age, to hang on tight to the horse's mane. This skill saved her life several times when she needed to flee from an approaching Confederate Army. Although years older, the sibling closest in age to Clara was Sally. She introduced Clara to literature and poetry.

When Clara turned four, she went to a two-term school session each of which lasted three months. Her teacher, Colonel Richard C. Stone, asked her to spell cat and dog—but she said she could spell "Artichoke." Mr. Stone then placed her in an advanced reading class.

In 1829, Clara's parents sent her to boarding school—but she was miserable and stopped eating so her teacher and the local doctor sent her home. By this time, her parents had bought a 300 acre farm. Clara and her four cousins, the Learneds—enjoyed playing in the wide-open spaces on the farm.

When Clara was eleven, her brother David fell from the top of a barn he was helping to build. So Clara quit school to stay home and care for him. She even applied loathsome leeches to drain off excess blood from his body. Later, a doctor advocated a steam-bath cure. That suggestion put an end to the leeches and David made a full recovery within three weeks.

Following David's recovery, thirteen-year-old Clara returned to her studies. Her teacher, Lucien Burleigh, gave her instruction in history, languages, English literature, and composition. The next year her teacher was Jonathon Dana; he gave her lessons in advanced philosophy, chemistry, and Latin. All Clara's teachers marveled at her diligence in studying and at her thirst for knowledge.

When school was out, Clara worked at her brother Stephen's mill. Since she was small, Stephen had to build a special little platform for his sister to stand on. She only worked there two weeks, however, when the mill burned to the ground.

Clara Barton, School Teacher

At the age of eighteen, Clara began teaching school. She had forty students and wore a new green dress designed to make her look older. The young teacher was nervous as she stood in front of her class made up of young children to boys a few years younger than she.

At recess, Clara joined the rowdier, older boys and participated in their sports and showed her athletic ability. "My four lads soon perceived that I was no stranger to their sports or their tricks." (2) Her students awarded her "high marks" for her ability.

Everywhere she taught, Clara not only disciplined her students, but taught them as well. When she was assigned to a school at Millward, however, Clara almost met her match. She tried at first to win over her students with smiles and kindness. But some of the bigger boys continued to disrupt the classroom. The ringleader of the disruptive group came to class late one morning. When he came in, he mocked Clara and upset the class, so Clara retrieved a riding whip from her desk, asked him to step forward and lashed him with the whip. She shocked the entire class with her actions. The young man stood up and apologized to his teacher. From then on, Clara was given problem schools to teach in; in general, she managed to discipline her students and still teach them the "three R's."

Her next venture was to teach at a public school in New Jersey where none had existed. Her school opened with six students to 600 a year later. But the school board demoted her to being only a school mistress, and put a man in charge of running the school. The demotion devastated Barton since she had developed and run the school for two years, then to have the board put a man in charge of the school because she was a mere woman. A short time later when she had an ailment of her vocal chords, she resigned teaching, never to teach again.

On to Washington, D.C.

In 1854, Clara to Washington, D.C. She hoped the milder climate would help her voice, and she ended up spending the next 60 years of her life in the city. Through Colonel Alexander Dewitt, a congressman and distant cousin from her home district, she found work in the Patent Office under Judge Charles Mason, the Commissioner of Patents. Most of the clerks were men, but Mason recognized Clara's superb work ethics and her fine handwriting. Clara became the first woman to work full time in the Patent Office. Before long, Mason promoted Clara to a position at the Confidential desk overseeing secret documents. Mason paid her the same salary as the men: $1400 per year—quite a lot of money at the time, especially for a woman. Some of the men were jealous of her and accused her falsely, but Mason put an end to it, firing the men.

Times began to change in Washington, and in the entire nation as tempers flared and fights even broke out between slavery and anti-slavery forces. When Abraham Lincoln was elected president in 1860 (1861), Clara Barton already had a good friend in Congress, Senator Henry Wilson, who would be much help to her later on. Lincoln even appointed Wilson Chairman of the Committee on Military Affairs.

Then, on April 12, 1861, when the south fired on Fort Sumter, the President declared war and asked for 75,000 soldiers to defend Washington, D.C. from rebels. Neighborhood groups of volunteer soldiers and militia arrived in Washington a few days later in response to Lincoln's summons. Included in the troops were forty young men in the Sixth Massachusetts Regiment who were former students of Clara Barton's. A short time later, as she tended wounded soldiers, Barton remarked in a letter to a friend, "So far as our poor efforts can reach, they shall never lack a kindly hand or a sister's sympathy if they come. In my opinion, this city will be attacked within the next sixty days...and when there is no longer a soldier's arm to raise the stars and stripes above our capitol, may God give strength to mine." (3)

Clara's relief efforts to the troops started soon after the influx of all the volunteers coming into Washington. Before long, she collected goods from churches, families and other groups. Her rented quarters in Washington began to overflow with clothing, bandages, jellies, liquors, preserves, medicines, and other supplies. Finally, she rented a warehouse, eventually filling three warehouses with supplies. Clara's sister, Sally, came to help her tend the wounded men near the capitol.

To the Front

After the battle of Fair Oaks on May 11, 1862, Barton learned of the 8,000 men wounded from the Battle. She quit her job at the Patent Office to better serve the troops. When she met with Colonel Daniel H. Rucker, assistant quartermaster general in charge of transportation, he gave her permission to have six wagons loaded with men and supplies to move to the front.

When she gathered all the necessary permits and passes, Clara was ready to travel to the battlefield. She wore a long, dark skirt, a plaid jacket and a kerchief over her hair. She arrived at Culpepper, Virginia, two days after the Battle of Cedar Mountain, on August 9, 1862. As her wagon came to the field hospital at midnight, Brigade Surgeon James L. Dunn was amazed to discover that Clara had brought bandages, dressings, and other supplies—all items the hospital had run out of. Dunn praised her, referring to her as an "angel sent from heaven."

As she ministered to the troops missing arms and legs, she gave them bread soaked in wine, and applesauce and soup. Other organizations, too had by this time been raised up to tend the wounded and dying men. After each battle when Clara's supplies were exhausted, she returned to the city to restock her supplies. Over and over Barton ministered to the wounded soldiers during the days of the war. She received much praise for her timely help and work following the war's major battles.

After Robert E. Lee surrendered at Appomattox on April 12, 1865, Clara found a new job. Under the authority of President Lincoln, she began to search for some 80,000 missing soldiers. Clara's forte' was setting up and organizing records, which she did.

Following her duties of locating missing soldiers, Barton began a series of lectures recounting her civil war experiences. She earned $75 to $100 for each lecture, taking in as much as $1000 some months. She needed the money since she had exhausted her own savings on provisions for the soldiers for whom she cared. Clara's lecture tour, although bringing in much needed monies, left her exhausted. Her doctor recommended a trip to Europe for rest and relaxation. She travelled with her sister Sally, at first to Glasgow, Scotland. From there, Clara went to Geneva, Switzerland, where she was approved by a group of Swiss dignitaries, including Doctor Louis Appia, who participated in establishing the International Red Cross.

After some time, during which Barton helped war victims in Europe, she returned to America where her doctor again prescribed rest. In the meantime, however, she was persuaded by Dr. Louis Appia to head up the International Red Cross in America. And, by May 21, 1881, after negotiations were completed with government officials, the American Red Cross was formed with Clara Barton as President.

Clara Barton's contributions to her country proved to be great. Her heroism during the civil war in reaching out to the dead and dying soldiers received much praise not only from officials above her, but from the soldiers to whom she ministered.

Her heroism also extended to founding the American Red Cross—surely this last, is a tribute to her courage and mercy to those suffering in time of war and tragedy. Truly, Clara Barton's legacy lives on during every kind of crisis in the U.S., and even world-wide when the Red Cross comes on the scene. Were she alive today, she would rejoice in what her vision has wrought.

Finally, whatever work God calls you to do, He will equip you and strengthen you for the task. Later on, you can say, "I have fought a good fight and have finished the race. I have kept the faith. Now there is in store for me the crown of righteousness, which the Lord, the righteous judge will award to me on that day" (2 Timothy 4:7-8, NIV). What a wonderful achievement—and you could not ask for a more blessed accolade.

CHAPTER SEVEN

Staying in Trust

**"I put Shelemiah, the priest, Zadok
the scribe, and a Levite named Pedaiah
in charge of the storerooms and made Hanan
son Zaccur, the son of Mattanaiah, their
assistant, because these men were considered
trustworthy. They were made responsible for
distributing the supplies to their brothers."
(Nehemiah 13:13, NIV)**

After Nehemiah had done considerable work in Jerusalem like
repairing the city wall, settling social injustices (such as the
poor not having enough food to eat), and registering those who
returned with Zerubbabel, the returning Jews celebrated the Feast
of Booths (Tabernacles) in Chapter 8:13-18.

This Festival is a festival of thanksgiving and certainly these
recent inhabitants of Jerusalem were thankful for what God had
done in restoring the walls of the city. They also dedicated the
walls. What a joyous occasion that must have been. Chapter
thirteen of Nehemiah takes place during Nehemiah's second
term as governor. Here, Nehemiah discovers that Eliashib, the
priest, had provided Tobiah, an Ammonite, a large room in the

Temple. When Nehemiah realized what Eliashib had done, he took immediate action and threw all of Tobiah's household goods out of the room—according to the law of Moses.

Then, Nehemiah discovered that the Levites had not been given their portion, and according to the law of Moses, they could not own land. To rectify this situation, Nehemiah appointed four "trustworthy" men as treasurers to monitor the tithes of grain, new wine, and other goods. These men were reliable, a synonym for being trustworthy. Nehemiah knew they would keep their word. He also knew these men would complete their work—and they would do a thorough job of keeping the records and other necessary bookkeeping.

You can learn from the example set by these men. In all your dealings with people, how important it is to keep your word (be dependable), to finish your work and do the best job you can.

Wilderness pioneer Daniel Boone blazed trails through the American wilderness thus helping many pioneers in their westward journey. Daniel first appeared in Berks County, Pennsylvania on November 2, 1734, the sixth child of Squire Boone and his wife's eleven children.

Squire Boone was a Quaker and married a Quaker woman by the name of Sarah Morgan. Squire also worked as a weaver, weaving wool, cotton, or linen, on a loom. By the time Daniel was born, his father had also set up a blacksmith's shop on his twenty-five acre homestead and grazed cattle.

Daniel, however, didn't care much for farming. His interests lay in the woods that surrounded the Boone property. He spent every spare minute exploring the outdoors. Because of his love of the outdoors, Daniel didn't spend much time in school; however, his knowledge of life in the woods was vast.

From the time of his youth, Daniel displayed much daring. This characteristic stayed with him throughout his life. He also refused to back down from a fight causing some dissension with other Quakers who were pacifists. Daniel's whole family agreed with Daniel about the restrictiveness of Quaker life. This disagreement with the Quakers resulted in their moving from Pennsylvania to North Carolina in 1748. In their new state they set up another homestead near the Yadkin River just on the edge of the frontier. The Boones were now in Indian territory belonging to the Cherokees and the Shawnees. Each of these tribes could attack at any time when threatened. Historian John Bakeless has suggested about the Boones: "The Boones were wanderers born. They had the itching foot….They heard of distant lands and knew that they must go there." (1)

As a young boy, Daniel made friends with the Indians and studied their ways. At the age of ten, Daniel's father bought twenty-five acres of wooded pasture. The land was some miles from the main farm, and Daniel spent the following six summers there with his mother where they tended the cattle. His father stayed home and managed the loom and blacksmith shop. Daniel's oldest sister took care of the younger children,

Daniel roamed the woods during the day while the cattle grazed, and at night he drove them home for milking. At thirteen, Daniel's father gave him a short-barreled, muzzle-loading rifle. Before long, he turned into an excellent marksman. He hunted deer, turkey, and bears with his (at that time) long-barreled flintlock. He could, according to legend, shoot a tick off a bear's snout at one hundred yards. Sometimes he stayed in the woods for weeks at a time. On the frontier, pioneers considered this time a "long hunt." Daniel returned with abundant hides and furs which made a profitable sale.

In 1754, British and French forces clashed on the western frontier. The first shots fired signaled the beginning of the French and Indian War. Not long after the outbreak of this war, Daniel met Rebecca Bryant and married her on August 14, 1756. The newlyweds moved into a cabin on Sugar Creek.

Before long, however, Daniel grew restless and wanted to leave because of settlers moving into the area and killing off the abundant game. But Rebecca refused, not wanting to leave family and friends. As it turned out, John Finley stopped by the Boone cabin in 1769. Finley had told Daniel earlier about the paradise of Kentucky.

So, on May 1, Daniel led Finley and four friends westward. The men journeyed through the Cumberland Gap on a Native American Trail called "The Warrior's Trace." Within a few weeks, Daniel stood atop a hill north of the Kentucky River. There, for the first time, he gazed at "The beautiful (land) of Kentucky." (2)

The Iroquois named the area "K a n t a ke," meaning "meadows." And, Boone, was not the first to see these bluegrass meadows. The Shawnee, Cherokee, and other tribes had blazed trails through the area for decades. For six months, Daniel's party hunted deer and trapped beaver.

But one day a Shawnee war party cornered Daniel and John Stevens, his brother-in-law. They took all the hides, plus the horses, but soon released the captives. It became a game as Daniel and John quickly recaptured the goods with the Shawnees taking them back. Ultimately, Boone and his brother-in-law escaped and had to begin trapping all over again.

By the time Daniel returned home, he was empty-handed; another war party had stolen his goods. Now, he was in debt. While in Kentucky, however, Daniel had studied the location of each hill, stream, and salt lick.

But now, Americans were pushing beyond the mountains, and in 1773, a wealthy Virginia landowner named William Russell wanted to explore Kentucky. He chose Daniel to lead his expedition. The expedition ended badly when a Delaware war party descended on the supply train headed up by James Boone,

Daniel's sixteen-year-old son. The warriors killed Boone and his friend, Henry Russell.

The entire expedition having lost heart, returned home. Daniel had to hunt all winter to feed his family. Daniel was now promoted to Militia Lieutenant, taking charge of several frontier forts. When the fighting ended with the Native Americans, Daniel was promoted to Captain.

Sometime later, Daniel and a number of workmen began to build a road into the Kentucky wilderness. The land lay between the Kentucky and Cumberland Rivers. On April 6, 1775, the road was finished, although most of the time it "was hilly, stony, or muddy." (3)

Daniel spent the rest of his days involved in many different exploits. He was heralded by the settlers' communities for his daring and for his craftiness in the woods. He was also respected by the Native Americans, like Blackfish, of the Shawnees, for his courage.

He sold off much of his land in order to be debt free. As he told his children, "He would rather be poor than retain an acre of land...so long as claims and debts hung over him." (4) Boone died on September 26, 1820 following a brief illness; but the stories and legends about him continue to grow until it becomes difficult to separate fact from fiction. Nevertheless, Boone's skills in the wilderness helped pave the way for the westward move of the settlers in the U.S. Without his skills, the frontier would have taken much longer to accomplish.

A person I know by the name of Larry, illustrates similar qualities to Daniel Boone. If I ask him to do something for me, he always keeps his word, however big or small the task he's been given. The work is done on time and he always does a thorough job. I can trust him. What a joy it is to work with people like Larry.

You can be like Larry, too. Apart from the Lord working in our lives, none of us can measure up to the Lord's standards. But He tells us over and over in His word in different places: "Call unto me, and I will answer thee, and show you great and mighty things, which thou knowest not" (Jer. 33:3, KJV).

And, the Lord always keeps His word.

CHAPTER EIGHT

Reproving Others

**"Faithful are the wounds of a friend;
but the kisses of an enemy are deceitful."
(Proverbs 27:6, KJV)**

As we look at this verse, the first person who comes to mind is Judas Iscariot. "He that betrayed him...saying, "Whomsoever I shall kiss, that same is he...And as soon as he was come, he goeth straightway to him, and saith, 'Master, master,' and kissed him" (Mark 14:44-46).

Jesus said of Judas earlier that it would have been better if he'd (Judas) never been born—and he is called the son of perdition, or the son of "Hell." Judas betrayed Jesus for 30 pieces of silver—hardly worthwhile when it cost him his eternal soul.

You can learn from Judas' life, though, as you consider your own life, and let the Lord examine you. Some areas you need to consider are: 1) to speak the truth in love, 2) to avoid evil companions, and 3) Pray for those in error. The apostle Paul confronted Peter in the book of Galatians about his not eating with the Gentiles, who were new Christian converts: "When Peter came to Antioch, I opposed him to his face, because he was clearly in the wrong. Before certain men came from James, he used to eat with the Gentiles. But when they arrived, he began to draw back and separate himself from the Gentiles {new Christians} because he was afraid of those who belonged to the circumcision group. The other Jews joined him in his hypocrisy, so that by their hypocrisy even Barnabas was led astray" (Gal. 2:11-13).

Here, Paul speaks the truth in love when he confronts Peter because of his being "two-faced." That is, believing one way and acting another. Once you're convinced that a brother or sister is in error, pray about it, then proceed to correct the person.

It's not easy to confront someone and say, "You are wrong to do this." It may cost you your friendship. But if you know your friend's words and actions don't line up with God's word, the Lord wants you to "speak the truth in love" to that person even as Paul did with Peter.

Another way you are to confront those in error is to pray for them. God wants His children to live upright lives. Sometimes, though, a fellow believer doesn't know what the Word teaches. Recently, I had to confront such a person. I chose to write a letter to him pointing out what the Scriptures teach—and used his own words to pinpoint his error. I have to leave the results with the Lord. I did what I believed the Lord wanted me to do. I will continue to pray for "Charles" and trust God to convict him of his sin.

Booker T. Washington was an African American who was born into slavery on a tobacco farm in Franklin County, Virginia on April 5, 1856 (Approx.). His mother, Jane, was the plantation cook, and his father was an unknown white man. Booker confessed that his "life had its beginning in the midst of the most miserable, desolate, and discouraging surroundings." (1) He knew little of his ancestry since slave records were not usually kept at that time. Booker never knew anything more about his father, finding little fault with him and seeing him as another victim of the "peculiar" institution of slavery.

Booker's living quarters (the cabin) also served as the Plantation kitchen. He and his two siblings, his brother, John, and sister, Amanda, slept side by side on a pallet of rags on the cabin's dirt floor.

One of Booker's early jobs at the Plantation was to haul corn to be ground to the mill. Someone would place the heavy bag on the back of the horse and the young boy would lead him to the mill. But often, the bag would fall off the horse, then Booker had to wait until a passer-by arrived to help him.

As far as family meal times, Booker recalls only that the children usually "picked up in whatever fashion they could: a piece of bread here, a scrap of meat there. They never sat down to eat a meal together as a family. Sometimes, too, "a portion of our family would eat from the skillet or pot, while someone else would eat from a tin plate, held on the knees." (2)

When he grew a little older, Booker was summoned to the "big house" at meal times to fan flies from the table by means of paper fans operated by a pulley. While he operated the pulley, the young boy absorbed the dinner table conversation which revolved around freeing the slaves and the war looming on the horizon. Even if one of the white masters was killed in the war, the slaves often felt grief and sadness, too.

The day the war ended, great rejoicing broke out at the Plantation. The news had been prepared for by the slaves for sometime as they gleaned information from the "grapevine telegraph." All the slaves were summoned to the "big house" to hear the important news: they were free, could go where they wanted to go, and do what they wanted to do. A stranger read a document to them (probably the Emancipation Proclamation) declaring their freedom. Intense gloom followed the rejoicing as the freed people began to wonder what to do.

The seventy or eighty-year-old slaves had already lived their most productive years. What could they do now? Some of the slaves elected to stay with their "old mar'sters" and "old missus" and arranged to do so. Many of the former slaves also determined to leave the plantation (at least for a few days) to know that they were really free, and second, they now must change their names. In Booker's case, his family moved to a place in West Virginia to join his stepfather, Washington Ferguson.

When Booker lived in West Virginia, the freed slaves had agreed to open a school and Booker looked forward to it eagerly. He worked at the time in a salt furnace and his stepfather realized that he brought in considerable money in his work, so he refused to let him go to school. The young boy was bitterly disappointed but did not give up on his dream.

Then Booker's mother stepped in. suggesting maybe he could work with the teacher in the evenings, which he did. Later on he was able to attend "day school," too, by working so many hours at the salt furnace before and after his classes. Booker also gave himself a name at the school: he had always been known as "Booker," so he kept that, but his mother said she had named him "Booker Taliaferro" when he was born, so he added that to the "Booker Washington," becoming Booker Taliaferro Washington.

One day while he was at work in the salt mine, Booker heard two men talking about a "great school for colored people" somewhere in Virginia. Then and there, he determined to go to the school. His plans to attend Hampton gained momentum when he found another job opportunity with a Mrs. Violet Ruffner. He did house cleaning for her, and although at first he feared being able to please her, he tried as hard as he could to do just that. After some time, Booker and Mrs. Ruffner "understood" each other, and he worked for her longer than anyone else—about a year and a half.

After that time, with few funds available, Booker set off for Hampton Institute—500 miles away. He walked, begged rides in wagons and somehow finally reached Hampton, but he was hungry, tired and dirty from his journey. Presenting himself to the head teacher for direction, he could see the disdain in her face for the way he appeared. After some time passed, the head teacher told the young man, "The adjoining recitation room needs sweeping. Take a broom and sweep it." (3)

Booker got to work sweeping the recitation room three times, dusting the woodwork around the walls, benches, tables, and desks three or four times. Then he reported back to the head teacher. She inspected his work and was very impressed. Afterward, she deemed him able to enter the institution. To Booker, his entrance into Hampton was a dream come true.

After graduating from Hampton in June, 1875, Booker went back to his home in Malden, Virginia, where he began teaching at the school for freed slaves and their children. He even included brushing teeth, washing hands and faces, and other hygiene good habits in the lesson schedule.

Sometime later, after Booker had returned to Hampton to do some teaching, he received an opportunity to go to Tuskegee (Alabama) to head up the Normal School for "Colored" students there. Booker was willing to try, although it was a tall order. Arriving at Tuskegee, the young teacher discovered a scarcity of buildings, teaching materials, but not students. So Booker had to locate suitable buildings, first of all, and next, obtain books and other teaching materials. In time, Booker was able to receive many donation and build up the school. The Tuskegee students themselves built many of the buildings as well as doing other work on the buildings.

Booker was quickly put in the position of raising money for the Institute. He traveled throughout the South giving speeches and raising funds for Tuskegee. Fortunately, in his days at Hampton, he had received some training in public speaking. When he was invited to speak at the Atlanta Cotton States International Exposition in Atlanta on September 18, 1895, he caused an uproar.

As he responded to the race question in his address, Booker advocated a "separate but equal" policy. He said, "In the future, in our humble way, we shall stand by you with a devotion that no foreigner can approach, ready to lay down our lives, if need be, in defense of yours…In all things that are purely social we can be as separate as the fingers, yet one as the hand in all things essential to mutual progress." (4)

Because of his being an outstanding teacher, writer and speaker on Black problems in the 19th century, his views were widely applauded at the time. Sometime later, other Black leaders like W.E.B. Du Bois, strongly criticized him. And in the 20th century, Civil Rights leaders took much exception to Booker's ideas.

Nevertheless, Booker T. Washington did much to assist the Black race following the Civil War. He also greatly promoted Black education through his efforts as a leader, teacher, and speaker at Tuskegee Institute largely because he was not afraid to solicit help for the school wherever he could find it. He lived an amazing life and pulled himself up by his bootstraps and endured much deprivation in his desire to get an education. His life was exemplary despite the criticism leveled against him after the Atlanta Cotton States Address in 1895. His dream was to better his own race and build up Tuskegee Institute—which to a great extent he did.

A final area you need to address is to make sure you associate with the right people. The Bible puts it this way: "Do not be mislead. 'Bad company corrupts good character.' Come back to your senses as you ought, and stop sinning" (1 Cor. 15:33, NIV).

A truth you can learn from this verse is that you become like the people with whom you associate. So, for your own good, as well as for the sake of the Gospel, be cautious about those with whom you associate. Try to be with upstanding, faith-filled people who seek to follow the Lord with their whole heart. If you associate with such people, you can never go wrong.

CHAPTER NINE

Conveying Truth

"For unless you are honest in small matters, you won't be in large ones. If you cheat even a little, you won't be honest with greater responsibilities. And if you are untrustworthy about worldly wealth, who will trust you with the true riches of heaven?"
(Luke 16: 10-12, TLB)

The first thing you can learn from this passage is Jesus' attitude toward money. Money is important, both in the secular realm and in the heavenly realm, and how you manage the money you have tells much about your values.

If you have a business, for example, you need a certain amount of money to manage it. You have certain people to pay every week, or month, and certain regular items to pay at the same time. I like to set up a budget so I know how much money is going out and how much is coming in. Even running a home is run on these same principles.

Whatever you do, if you lack money to pay your bills, being dishonest and cheating will not be the right way to handle the situation. Pray and ask God for wisdom to know what to do. James tells us in James 1:5-6: "If you want to know what God wants you to do, ask him, and he will gladly tell you, for he is always ready to help you."

As you learn to manage the money God has given you, always remember to take out your tithes first. Even if you don't much to give, give what you can and pray God's blessings on it. The Lord will multiply it back to you. Another way to be more thrifty with your finances is to pare down your expenses. Determine which items are necessities—and which are not. Sometimes utilities will offer special discounts on "bundling" your services. That can be a way to save. Just go over each item in your budget and ask God to help you. You'll be amazed at how much you can save in your budget. Even John D. Rockefeller kept track of every penny he spent and every penny he earned. He said God gave him the gift of managing money. And, indeed, he did!

In this passage in Luke, the accountant has stolen from his employer and the employer is about to fire him. So the accountant quickly settles the outstanding accounts at half their value. His employer was impressed with his shrewdness, but at the same time, he could not condone his earlier stealing/cheating from his employer.

What you can learn from this account is the importance of being honest and living above reproach. Even if no one else sees you, the Lord sees you: "For the eyes of the Lord search back and forth across the whole earth, looking for people whose hearts are perfect toward him, and that he can show his great power in helping them" (2 Chronicles 16:9, TLB).

Davy Crockett, an American Frontier trail blazer, died defending the Alamo in Texas. Crockett's feats have given rise to many legends: How he killed a bear when he was three years old; how he "grinned" down savage animals armed only with his strong grip and abundant charm; and how he never failed to hit a bull's eye with "Ol' Betsey," his long rifle (1) Some of these legends were true, some were not. But he was a trail-blazing pioneer of the vanishing frontier and an excellent marksman.

Davy Crockett was born on a farm on Big Limestone Creek in Greene County, Tennessee on August 17, 1786. His ancestors came from Irish stock, settling in North Carolina before the American Revolution. Davy's grandfather, David Crockett, moved onto the frontier in Eastern Tennessee in the 1770's where warring Indians killed him. Davy also had eight brothers and sisters.

His father operated a tavern (after failing as a hog farmer and miller) on the wagon road between Knoxville, Tennessee, and Abingdon, Virginia. The tavern also doubled as an Inn where wagon drivers could spend the night sleeping three and four to a bed. Davy relished listening to all the "tall tales" of the travelers who stayed at the tavern. In fact, he began developing his own "tall tales."

As he grew, Davy also developed his skills as a woodsman and hunter. He became renowned for being a crack shot. He was able to shoot the wick off a candle at 300 feet; and once killed 47 bears in a single month.

At thirteen, Davy's father wanted him to go to school. Before long, however, he made a powerful enemy in the school bully. In order to escape his father's punishment for scratching the boy's face, as Davy said, "I scratched his face all to a flitter jig," he ran away to Virginia. (2) He soon found work as a farmhand and received a small compensation.

When he reached the age of 18, however, Davy wanted to get married. Unfortunately, he had a couple of unhappy romances— that is, the girl ended up with someone else. After the second romantic breakup, Davy wrote, "My heart was bruised, and my spirits were broken down." (3)

Things worked out for Davy, though, when he met Polly (Mary) Finley in 1806 at a community dance party. This time, everything happened in his favor. Polly had broken up with another young man so she could marry Davy. Just before he met her, however, he decided to return to school so he could at least learn to read and write. He was already eighteen, but realized his need for some schooling. He stayed at his studies for six months, then left school for good. In just a few months after they met, Polly and Davy were married. They soon had two sons, John Wesley and William Crockett, and a daughter, Margaret. Davy's crack marksmanship kept the family well supplied with deer, rabbits, and other small game.

In 1813, Creek Warriors, or "Red Sticks" as the settlers called the Creek Indians, went on the war path south of the Crockett's Elk River County. However, when a Red Stick war party crashed Fort Mims in Alabama and massacred more than 500 settlers, the whites organized a militia with General Andrew Jackson in command. Davy signed up to be a militia scout, and though he didn't distinguish himself in that role, his storytelling amused everyone, including General Jackson.

Davy continued his days as an explorer and frontiersman; he wasn't cut out to be a farmer. Before long, though, he did venture into politics. He became a magistrate and Justice of the peace. Soon, the local militia elected him as their colonel. Then some of his friends persuaded Davy to run for the Tennessee State Legislature. All he knew to do for speeches was to tell his humorous, folksy stories when asked to give a speech. Following the speech, he offered the hard-working farmers free drinks at the liquor stand. Davy's opponents followed him to the "stump," but usually the crowd had dispersed by then—and Davy ended up winning the election by a landslide. He ran and lost a subsequent election bid and returned to his real loves: hunting and following new wilderness ventures.

Davy was in and out of politics for a few years, even serving in national politics, but afterward, he always returned to his roots of hunting and exploring the wilderness. His next venture lay in the Texas wilderness. Texas lay outside U.S. boundaries, and Davy hoped for a new beginning for his life. However, Texas was controlled by Mexico. Many of the American-born residents clamored for independence from Mexico.

The situation between the Americans and the Mexicans finally culminated at the Alamo, formerly an old Spanish mission. Davy Crockett was among the Americans in the Alamo as they fought for an independent Texas. So, on February 23, 1836, Santa Ana, the Mexican leader vowed the Americans "would be given no quarter" but would "be killed to the last man"—the Texans remained firm. (4) The Alamo defenders ultimately lost the battle due to low ammunition and fewer fighting men. On March 6, as the last defender was slain, the Mexicans gained control of the Alamo.

Davy Crockett was one of the last defenders to die, according to legend. His gun, Ol' Betsey, was found "bloodied and broken from the final moments of hand-to-hand fighting." (5) To the end, however, Davy Crockett retained a fighting spirit. His love of adventure and the wilderness made him a perfect man for the time he lived in. His favorite saying, reflecting his back woods' simplicity and honesty was, "Be always sure you're right, then go ahead." (6)

A final point to remember is to complete your work to the best of your ability and finish it in a timely fashion. To do a good job always pleases the Lord. He is a "rewarder of them that diligently seek Him" (Hebrews 11:6). May God give you much favor as you practice these things.

CHAPTER TEN

Maintaining a Faithful Walk

**"How can a young man keep his way pure?
By living according to your word.
I have hidden your word in my heart
that I might not sin against you."
(Psalm 119:9-11, NIV)**

These verses sum up the Christian life and tell the Christian how to live. Further, everything in these verses points to God's Word as being the key to a successful Christian life. Back in Joshua, the Lord reminds Joshua, too, how to live a God-centered life. Thus, in Joshua 1:8, the Bible says, "Do not let this Book of the Law depart from your mouth; meditate on it day and night, so that you may be careful to do everything written in it. Then you will be prosperous and successful."

In the Old Testament, the Lord tells the people, "These commandments that I give you today are to be upon your hearts. Impress them on your children. Talk about them when you sit at home and when you walk along the road, when you lie down and when you get up. Tie them as symbols on your hands and bind them on your foreheads. Write them on the door frames of your houses and on your gates" (Deut. 6:6-9, NIV).

By having these constant reminders of the Word before them, the people of God would know what to do at all times. Of course, in the Old Testament, the way of salvation came by the people adhering to the Law of Moses. In the New Testament, John tells us, "The law was given by Moses, grace and truth came by Jesus Christ—who is our righteousness" (John 11:17, NIV).

Through these verses, you learn the importance of studying the Word on a regular basis. A Christian will not grow very much apart from studying the Word. In fact, the Word provides his spiritual food. It leads and guides us and shows us what to do. The time spent reading the Bible doesn't have to be long, but a Christian should read it daily until it speaks to him.

The second discipline the Christian needs is prayer. The apostle Paul urges a Christian to "pray without ceasing." I believe that means to keep the Lord uppermost in your mind. Prayer is really the answer to everything in the Christian life. If you're trying to determine God's will about something, claim the promises of God and He will show you what to do. In Colossians 3:15, Paul urges the believer to "Let the peace of Christ rule in your hearts." God's peace in our hearts acts as an "Umpire," filtering out evil thoughts and ideas.

George Mueller, a wonderful man of God, lived in England in the 1800's and supported numerous orphanages through prayer alone. He didn't believe in asking anyone but God concerning his needs. He said Christians fail in prayer because they don't "persist" until the answer comes. That doesn't mean praying the same thing over and over, but thanking God for the answer once you have a promise from Him.

Christians should also confess any sin that has crept into their lives. First John 1:9 is a good verse to claim for this. God has forgiven ALL your sins in Christ and His righteousness, but like Peter, when Jesus washed his feet and Peter said, "Wash me all over," but the Lord said that wasn't necessary because he was already clean (John 13:5-11). Because Peter walked in the world, only his feet needed cleansing. You can confess sins of "omission and commission" since that's where many of us fall short. In other words, don't let sin build up in your life.

George Washington Carver was an amazing man. Even as a baby, he should not have lived except that God's hand was on him. In 1864, George Carver experienced a tumultuous beginning: when he was just a few weeks old, he and his mother, Mary, were kidnapped by "bush whackers" —night raiders during the Civil War era near Diamond, Missouri. The raiders knew the slave Mary would bring a good price, but the baby was tiny and sickly-looking, so they kept Mary and dropped the little baby by the roadside. Fortunately for baby George, his owner, Moses Carver, came looking for the baby and his mother. He recovered only baby George.

The Carvers were kind people and loved George and his five-year-old brother, Jim. And on December 18, 1865, the 13th Amendment to the Constitution went into effect, so the Carvers decided to raise the boys as their own children. Though it was unusual for white parents to raise Black children, the neighbors respected Moses Carver because of his prosperity. Moses raised race horses that he trained for future track racing.

George remembered the Carvers as loving parents; he also said, "There are so many things, that naturally, I erased from my mind. There are so many things that an orphan child does not want to remember." (1) George's big brother, Jim, helped Moses with the demanding work in the fields, while George a frail and sickly little boy, helped Mrs. Carver in the kitchen with cooking meals, mending clothes, and tending the garden.

Early on, George showed a special interest in the plants he tended. He experimented with a variety of soils and growing conditions. Local people soon called him the "Plant Doctor" and sought his advice on growing their own plants and flowers. The

Carvers encouraged George's rare gift and talents as the young boy explored the nearby fields and woods collecting various specimens of many plants and creatures.

After encountering some of George's live specimens, however, Mrs. Carver made sure he emptied his pockets before coming into the house. George said about the early days of his life, "I wanted to know every strange stone, flower, insect, bird, or beast." (2) The only reference book available at the time was *Webster's Elementary Spelling Book,* a book that didn't begin to satisfy George's advanced questions.

George and his brother Jim went to church regularly, and by the time he was ten, George had become a Christian. Throughout his life he believed first and foremost that God created everything—he linked his views of nature to his belief in God as the Creator.

Before the Civil War, laws prohibited teaching slaves to read and write. After the war ended in 1865, however, Jim and George enrolled in a local school that met in the church where they worshipped. The school turned them away later because they were black. In 1876, the Carvers provided a tutor for George backing up his desire to learn. But the tutor didn't have the knowledge to satisfy him. He tried other nearby schools, finally ending up in Fort Scott, Kansas. Then, after a violent episode involving a rape charge concerning a Black man and subsequent hanging, George fled the town in fear.

At that time, he traveled to various places (and schools) in Kansas, supporting himself with the domestic skills he learned from Mrs. Carver. By 1885, George was ready for college, and once more, had trouble finding a college that would accept him.

In the meantime, George became a homesteader and claimed 160 acres of land under the Homestead Act of 1862. He built himself a sod house and added a conservatory filled with native plants. However, he became frustrated by the effects of the climate on the vegetables and other crops he planted. The winters were harsh on his crops—especially when water was scarce. Finally, he gave up being a homesteader and left Ness County in 1889.

From Ness County, George traveled to Winterset, Iowa, and then to Ames, Iowa, where he entered the Iowa State College of Agriculture and Mechanical Arts. Prior to his enrollment, George had participated in the art department. He painted many fine pictures of horticultural subjects; ultimately, though, he knew it would be hard to support himself as an artist.

One professor said of George, "Carver is by all means the ablest student we have." (3) The professor referred in part to George's ability to graft plants, to cross-fertilize plants (combining cells from two different plants), and to create hybrids (cross-fertilizing different plants to form new ones). George graduated in 1894 with a bachelor of agriculture degree.

In March, 1896, he received a letter from Booker T, Washington, Principal of the Tuskegee Institute in Alabama inviting George to be on the faculty there. He wanted him to head up the school's new agriculture department. George accepted the offer from Washington and plunged into his work. Tuskegee's agricultural experimental station, which was just ten acres, thrived under Carver's direction. He was concerned, however, with the worn-out condition of much soil in the South from repeated plantings of cotton. He said, "The average farmer goes on trying to raise cotton in the same old way, which means nothing but failure, more or less, for him." (4) The solution, for Carver, was threefold: 1) Crop rotation to enrich the soil, 2) The use of organic fertilizer to replace the soil's lost nutrients, and 3) The introduction of new crops that farmers could sell on the market as well as serve at their own kitchen tables.

As they implemented these ideas, the students planted crops such as peanuts, sweet potatoes, black-eyed peas, alfalfa, velvet beans, and soy beans. Carver also took his agricultural knowledge to the rural poor farmer in the South. Whatever means he could use to help the poor Southern farmer, Carver attempted. He set up his own laboratory early on in Tuskegee. One of the products he made was "peanut milk," better known now as "peanut butter." In fact, Carver came up with a whole list of uses for the peanut: Peanut milk, Peanut candy, Instant coffee, Cosmetics, and Breakfast food.

The rest of Carver's days after age 60 were packed full of conducting experiments, teaching classes, and giving speeches all over the country. He was truly a great scientist and a great American who never stopped growing mentally and spiritually. As Henry Ford, a good friend of Carver's, said in 1942, "In my opinion, Professor Carver has taken Thomas Edison's place as the world's greatest living scientist." (5)

George Washington Carver accomplished many things with a life that started out with so little promise. Although Tuskegee Institute boasts a monument of Carver on its grounds, the greatest monument is the man himself: his life and a legacy that will remain forever.

One last troublesome area for the Christian is taking offense. The Christian is to walk in love toward others—especially fellow believers. Jesus says in the Scriptures that "offenses will come"— but you don't have to let them stay! Be sure to confess them and repent of them quickly, so your relationship with the Lord is not broken.

So, these are the main requirements for the Christian life: 1) Read the Word regularly 2) Pray without ceasing, and 3) Stay free of taking offenses. If you practice these disciplines faithfully, your Christian life will prosper and you'll be filled with peace and joy!

The Blessings of Giving Thanks

(The Art of Thanksgiving)

The Bible urges the Christian to be thankful at all
times and in all things. As it says in Ephesians 5:20:
"Giving thanks always for all things
unto God and the Father
in the name of our Lord Jesus Christ."

Father, with everything else You've given me,
Grant me a grateful heart.

Giving Thanks

For three things I thank God every day of my
Life:
Thanks that he has vouchsafed me
knowledge of His works;
deep thanks that he has set
in my darkness the lamp of faith;
deep, deepest thanks that I have
another life to look forward to--
a life joyous with light and flowers
and heavenly song.
Helen Adams Keller

Lord,
Teach me to count my blessings—
Large and small.

Meditations on Thankfulness

(Eight days of Inspiration
Derived from the Word "Thankful")

Sunday
T IS FOR THANKSGIVING

Giving thanks always for all things unto God.
Ephesians 5:20

The blessedness of giving thanks to the Lord cannot be overemphasized. Whatever the situation, whether it be filled with joy, or filled with sadness and even despair, we are told to give thanks to God.

Why does the Bible tell us to do such a simple yet often difficult task? To give God thanks, first of all, is an act of worship and obedience—we are commanded to do so. But giving thanks also implies trust in God; trust that He will do what His Word promises; trust that He will answer that seemingly impossible prayer request; and trust that "all things work together for good" (Romans 8:28).

Throughout the Old Testament, particularly in the Psalms, we are told repeatedly to give thanks and praise to God. A good example of this instruction appears in Psalm 50:14-15 where the Psalmist reminds us to "Offer unto God thanksgiving, and pay thy vows unto the most High. And call upon me in the day of trouble: I will deliver thee, and thou shalt glorify me." Here we see a direct link between giving thanks to God, calling upon Him in trouble, and then, witnessing His mighty deliverance in and through a difficult place.

When Shadrach, Meshach, and Abednego refused to bow down and worship an earthly king, they were thrown into the fiery furnace. But they trusted God to deliver them—and He did! In fact, they came out of the intense fire and heat without their bodies or clothing being burned, without their hair being singed or even the smell of smoke clinging to them!

As we give thanks to God, something mysterious happens. It is as though we place our hand in His and provide an open door for Him to work. May the Lord help us to be thankful at all times.

Monday

H IS FOR HEART

I will praise thee, O Lord,
With my whole heart;
I will show forth all thy marvelous works.
Psalm 9:1

The psalmist's joy in praising the Lord is contagious as he determines to praise the Lord with his whole heart. In essence, the psalmist makes a vow to praise God whether anyone else does or not. Neither will he consider his feelings nor his emotions in the matter; but he will put forth strength of his will in this high calling of praise.

With enthusiasm, the psalmist also declares that by his will he should be enabled to give whole-hearted praise to the Lord; no half-hearted measures are sufficient. If an athlete running a race wants to win, he must run with his whole being set on the goal. Otherwise, any halfhearted effort guarantees failure. Moreover, whatever occupation a person has, he must pursue it wholeheartedly, or he will not be successful. Would we desire to have a surgeon operate on us if he would not do his best? Or would we have an attorney represent us if he possessed an indifferent attitude? No, whatever our task, we need to do it with quiet determination, yet with confidence and joy knowing that we have done our best.

So with the psalmist, there is no proper way to praise the Lord except with a "whole heart." Having made this declaration, the psalmist adds that he will then show forth all of God's marvelous works.

What are these marvelous works? They're simply God's dealings with each of us, beginning with the work of Christ's salvation. But daily we see the Lord's provision for us in many things: a good night's rest, strength for the day, His watch-care over us from harm, our daily bread, family and friends, and overall, His peace and joy.

May the Lord grant us grace to praise Him with our whole heart—and thus to show forth His marvelous works.

Tuesday

A IS FOR ACCEPTABLE

Let the words of my mouth, and the meditation
of my heart, be acceptable in thy sight,
O Lord, my strength, and my redeemer.
Psalm 19:14

The psalmist prays that his words and his thought will find favor with the Lord. He knows what we all know too well—that we often speak without thinking; but once we utter the words, we can never call them back. Like flying arrows, they go straight to the mark—whether for good or for ill.

Knowing too well the problem of "taming the tongue," the psalmist cries out to God for help. He does not want to be guilty of hidden and unconscious faults, nor of presumptuous sins (or willful sins). On the one hand, he speaks of unknown sins; on the other, he addresses the sins he's aware of committing but seems helpless to prevent. He is painfully aware of the too-frequent hypocrisy in his life. For example, he meets a fellow Christian and calls to him, "Good afternoon, Brother Bill. How good it is to see you!" But under his breath he thinks, "That old reprobate. I hope our paths don't cross again!" His attitude and words are hypocritical and contradict the clear teaching of biblical verses such as I Peter 1:22 that says to have "unfeigned love of the brethren."

It's easy for us to identify with the psalmist since we, too, want to say and do the right thing. Because of his sinful nature, however, the psalmist knows he cannot attain to what the Scripture commands by himself. But he rejoices at the close of Psalm 19 as he calls upon the Lord, "my strength and my redeemer." The Lord can—and will—help him overcome his hypocritical ways. As he seeks the Lord for help, the Lord will render his words and his thoughts acceptable in His sight.

Lord, help us to pray this prayer today—and mean it!

Wednesday

N IS FOR NAME

O Lord, our Lord, how excellent is thy name
in all the earth!
Psalm 8:1

If we ask, "What's in a name?" we might get many different answers. Most of us understand, however, that the name of a person represents all that he or she is. The person who bears a certain name is distinct. No other individual is identical to that person.

So it is with God; only His name is high above every other name on earth or in heaven. Further, the psalmist declares the Excellency of the Lord's name and stresses that God has set His glory (and his name) above the heavens. We see God's glory everywhere in creation: in the beauty of a sunrise and sunset; in the wonder of a budding flower; in the music of a bird's song; in the uniqueness of other people; and throughout this beautiful world that He has made.

When we speak of the meaning of God's name, consider what the Scripture says: "His name shall be called Wonderful, Counselor, The Mighty God, The Everlasting Father, The Prince of Peace" (Isaiah 9:6); "Thou shalt call his name JESUS: for he shall save his people from their sins" (Matthew 1:21); "They shall call his name Emmanuel, which being interpreted is, God with us" Matthew 1:23). Also, in the New Testament, Jesus declares, "Before Abraham was, I am" (John 8:58). Last of all in the book of Revelation, the Lord says He is "Alpha and Omega, the beginning and the end," and the "KING OF KINGS, AND THE LORD OF LORDS."

The amazing fact about the names of the Lord is that He includes us in many of them—and He invites us to use His name in prayer. Truly, He is "God with us."

How thankful we should be to our gracious God for all He has provided for every need; for the wonder of His creation; and that He bids us to "Call upon My name!"

Thursday

K IS FOR KEEP

The Lord...will not suffer thy foot to be
moved: he that keepeth thee will not slumber.
Behold, he that keepeth Israel shall neither
slumber nor sleep. The Lord is thy keeper.
Psalm 121:2-5

Psalm 121 could well be known as the "Keeping Psalm." In fact, nearly every verse in this reassuring psalm uses the word "keep" in one way or the other. To "keep" something implies faithfulness and reliability; the word also speaks of preserving, as in the process of canning fruits and vegetables so they will last a long time.

The psalmist rests secure in the knowledge that God, the Maker of heaven and earth, is watching over him and protecting him. And he has that bedrock assurance that the Lord "orders" every step he takes. None of his footsteps will slip or slide because the Lord holds his feet to the path mapped out for him. Sometimes we think we have missed the way, but as we call on the One Who never slumbers nor sleeps, He will set our feet back on the right pathway. Even as Jonah got on the ship bound for Tarshish and the Lord sent a whale to transport him to Ninevah, the Lord will do the same for us to assure the finishing of our course.

The Lord not only keeps us, but He is our Keeper. The God of the universe has a personal interest in us. Like a gardener tending

81

his garden, the word "keeper" suggests the Lord taking care of every detail that concerns us. In a sense, we are His "keepsakes"! He makes sure the sun does not shine too brightly, nor the moon hide any treachery from us. In short, whether we're coming or going on our daily journey, the Lord oversees every aspect, protecting and caring for us.

Lord, teach us always to lift our eyes to You—from whence our help comes.

Friday

F IS FOR FAITHFULNESS

Thy mercy, O Lord, is in the heavens: and thy
faithfulness reacheth unto the clouds.
Psalm 36:5

Faithfulness is such a wonderful quality! We prize this characteristic in people above all others. To illustrate, if someone asks a woman to help in a community effort, usually the person who asks her knows she can count on her to fulfill her duties. She already knows the woman to be dependable and reliable; she is faithful. Or, if an organization wants a man to contribute his expertise to a small building project, the committee knows they can depend on him to be there because he said he would be. He keeps his word.

So it is with God. In this verse, the psalmist reaches for the clouds to extol God's faithfulness to us: God's love and faithfulness have no limit. Despite our sinfulness, God's mercy extends way past the sin as His love and compassion toward us attain the very heavens.

The prophet Jeremiah, in Lamentations 3:22-23, declares triumphantly: "It is of the Lord's mercies that we are not consumed, because his compassions fail not. They are new every morning: great is thy faithfulness." What confidence we can have toward the Lord as these words grip us. Even when we say or do wrong things, the Lord's hand is always outstretched toward us.

We serve a God whose love is steadfast and unchanging toward us, and we can rest in that knowledge.

May the Lord help us to be worthy recipients of His faithfulness to us.

Saturday

U IS FOR UNDERSTANDING

How sweet are thy words unto my taste!
yea, sweeter than honey to my mouth.
Through thy precepts I get understanding:
therefore I hate every false way.
Psalm 119:103-104

The psalmist had learned the secret of meditating in God's Word. To him, the book of the Law was not just another book, but its words contained the very life of God. Thus Jesus reminds us in John 6:63: "The words that I speak unto you, they are spirit, and they are life."

These words follow an earlier passage in which Jesus calls Himself "the Bread of Life." In these verses, Jesus, like the psalmist, lets us know the true worth of God's Word.

As He contrasts God's Word with natural food, Jesus illustrates the difference between the flesh and the spirit: Feeding the one leads to death; feeding the other leads to life. Moreover, He teaches us in Matthew 4:4: "It is written Man shall not live by bread alone, but by every word that proceedeth out of the mouth of God." Jesus answered Satan with these words when the devil commanded Him to turn stones into bread after Jesus' forty-day fast; thus, He provides an example for us to follow.

The psalmist, too, extols his love for God's Word. Through his maturity in the Lord, he can now truthfully exclaim that God's words are "sweeter than honey to my mouth!" Thinking of how sweet honey is on a slice of warm toast or topping cereal in a bowl, we can appreciate what he is saying. When he began his Christian life, he enjoyed the "milk" of God's Word, but now the Word constitutes his "daily bread" and even dessert!

Through his meditation in God's Word, the psalmist has received instruction as well as nourishment. This instruction in guidance, direction, correction, and encouragement shows him how to live according to God's will. By following God's Word, he can avoid the pitfalls of life (every false way)—or anything that would take him from the path the Lord has for him. By meditating in these truths, the psalmist grows in his understanding of how to conduct his life.

Lord, let Your Word become increasingly sweet to us, and enable us to grow in grace, in knowledge, and in our understanding of You.

Sunday

L IS FOR LIGHT

*The Lord is my light and my salvation; whom
shall I fear? The Lord is the strength of my
life; of whom shall I be afraid?*
Psalm 27:1

This verse expresses great hope and encouragement. The psalmist
tells of his personal relationship with the Lord when he says He
is "my light" and "my salvation." At the new birth, we discover a
new light in our lives—a new "lightness," peace, and joy in our
hearts. We know that God is real, and that He cares for us. But
that is just the beginning of the Christian life. Every step of the
way, God shines light on the believer's path. Because of God's
light, darkness and gloom disappear; they cannot remain in His
glorious light.

Can you remember being afraid of the dark when you were
a child? You'd thrust your body down under the sheets, then
you'd pull the covers up over your head. Somehow you thought
the darkness would leave if you couldn't see it. But if you poked
your head out, the darkness was still there.

Growing up we are taught that darkness hides all manner of
evil. But in and of ourselves, we are helpless to dispel the darkness
until our Savior comes to live in our hearts. Light, especially
sunlight, is the most important energy in the world. Without
it, trees, plants, and flowers could not grow, nor many animals
find food and shelter. Even as human beings, we require essential

vitamins found in the sun's rays. When we have rainy weather and the sun doesn't shine for days, the farmer's crops are in danger.

How comforting to know that God's light will never dim nor go out, and that we can always walk in its brightness. In addition, Jesus says in John 8:12: "I am the light of the world: he that followeth me shall not walk in darkness, but shall have the light of life." No wonder the psalmist can rejoice in the God Who is not only his Light, but his Salvation. From start to finish, he has nothing to fear. Thus the psalmist dreads nothing; he finds shelter and safety in the Lord.

How thankful we are that the Lord is our light and our salvation. May we live today in the strength of this knowledge.

References

Chapter One
God's Salesman. Carol V.R. George. Oxford University Press, 1993; pp. 15, 61, 62, 63, 66.

Chapter Two
Andrew Carnegie. John S. Bowman. Silver Burdett Press, Simon & Schuster. 1989, p. 28.

Investing Famous Fortunes. Books for Libraries Press, 1931; p. 131.

Chapter Three
Cyrus McCormick and The Mechanical Reaper. Leah J. Aldrich. Morgan Reynolds Publishing, Inc. Greensboro, NC, 2002; pp.9, 11, 12, 16.

Icons of Invention, Vol. I. John W. Klooster, 2009; pp. 28, 28, 51, 52; 2009.

Chapter Four
Abraham Lincoln, The Writer: A Treasury of His Greatest Speeches and Letters. Compiled and edited by Harold Holzer. Boyd Mills Press, Honesdale, PA, 2000, p. 4.

Abraham Lincoln. Janis Herbert, Chicago Review Press, Inc. 2007; pp. 8, 8, 16, 39.

Chapter Five
Dale Carnegie: The Man Who Influenced Millions. Giles Kemp and Edward Claflin. St. Martin's Press, New York, 1989, p. 2.

How to Win Friends and Influence People. Dale Carnegie, Simon & Schuster, New York, N.Y., 2009; pp. 243, 17, 21, 45, 159.

Chapter Six
Clara Barton. Susan E. Hamen. ABDO Publishing Co., Edina, MN, 2010; pp. 17, 29, 43.

Chapter Seven
Daniel Boone: Wilderness Pioneer. Wm. R. Sanford & Carl R. Green. Enslow Publishers, Springfield, NJ, 1997; pp. 9, 17, 24, 36.

Chapter Eight
Up From Slavery. Booker T. Washington. Random House, NY, 1999; pp. 3, 8, 35, 144, 145.

Chapter Nine
Davy Crockett. Daniel E. Harmon. Chelsea House Publishers. Stockton, NJ, 2002; pp. 18, 11, 17, 56, 57, 59.

Chapter Ten
George Washington Carver: Botanist and Ecologist. Chelsea House Publishers, 1984; pp. 10, 12, 13, 26, 33, 70.

The Sinners' Prayers

For God so loved the world, that he gave his only begotten Son, that whosoever believeth in him should not perish, but have everlasting life (John 3:16)

On the cross of Calvary, God's mighty love was revealed and offered unconditionally to all who would be saved. This love gift of God is eternal life through Jesus Christ our Lord.

So little time is left before Jesus Christ comes back! Are you ready for His return? If not, I would like to help you do just that. For the wages of sin is death; but the gift of God is eternal life through Jesus Christ our Lord (Romans 6:23).

The exciting news is this very moment, you can receive Christ's gift of everlasting life by faithfully praying this simple prayer from your heart today!

Heavenly Father, in the name of Jesus Christ your Son whom you sent to this world to die and completely pay for all sins,- I acknowledge that I am a sinner in need of a saviour. I confess and repent of all my sins and ask you to forgive and remove all my sins with the blood of Jesus Christ, which was shed for the remission of sins. I receive in confidence that forgiveness from all my sins now in the name of Jesus Christ. Amen. I confess with my mouth that Jesus is Lord and I believe in my heart that God raised him from the dead. I therefore receive into my heart Jesus Christ as my personal Lord and Saviour. Thank you for saving me in the name of Jesus Christ. Amen!

Welcome:

If you prayed this prayer, then congratulations and welcome to the family of God. Please write or call us today so that we can send you more information on how to build your new life in God through our Lord Jesus Christ.

God Bless You in the Name of Jesus Christ our Lord and Personal Saviour. Amen!

For more information, contact

Rev. Prayer Kenneth Obadoni
115 William Stephenson Drive
Whitby ON, Canada
www.seedsoutreach.org
rev.pobadoni@seedsoutreach.org
905 706 0944

OTHER BOOK WRITTEN BY THE AUTHOR:

SHAKE YOURSELF LOOSE.

The Author

Rev. Prayer Kenneth Obadoni is the founder and pastor of Seeds of Knowledge Outreach Ministries.

Non-denominational outreach ministry currently based in Whitby, Ontario Canada.

Rev. Prayer is a teacher of God's word with viable proofs in the lives of men and woman.

Married to his amiable wife Lydia Oristeweyinmi Adodo-Obadoni, they make their home in Whitby, ON, Canada.